Traveller's Joy

LIVING & WALKING ON THE ISLE OF WIGHT

by
RON WINTER

with photography by
PAT WINTER

Acknowledgements

The authors wish to express their gratitude to the
many good people who have helped in one way
or another in the construction of this book.
Particular thanks are due to Mrs. Sandell of
Newchurch Post Office for the picture on page 8,
and to Mrs. Marjorie Blamey. Marjorie Blamey
is the artist responsible for all the delightful
flower studies used to embellish each walk.
These have a character all their own , and adorn
the pages just as Travellers Joy adorns the ways
and hedges.

First published in 1993 by Forget-me-not Books
and The Manor Design & Printing Partnership
ISBN 1 870374 150

Text © C.W.R.Winter 1993
Photographs © P.Winter 1993

Book Design and Production
The Manor Design & Printing Partnership
Whitwell, Isle of Wight, England

Introduction

The plant 'Traveller's Joy' was given its name by John Gerard, the 16th century botanist, because it was to be found 'decking and adorning ways and hedges where people travel'. It is a beautiful and prolific plant and we could not think of a better name for our book, which was born of the joy we had in travelling 'the ways and hedges' of the Isle of Wight.

You have only to get off the roads and away from the motor cars and transistor radios to find so many beautiful wild flowers that the mind boggles. We have brought you pictures of some of these, in the hope that they will whet your appetite for more, and have tried to tell you of some of the many other interesting things in this historic and heritage-rich Island.

None of the walks is very long or arduous, though we did on several occasions climb the Downs, which may temporarily tire the legs but permanently uplift the spirit. Some of the walks however are along the old disused railway tracks where the going is flat, and all the time we kept in mind the possibility of wheel chairs being able to negotiate them, for we would dearly love to share the delights we enjoyed with those who cannot walk at all.

So even if you are confined to the house we hope there is something in this book to interest you and bring a breath of the countryside into your life. To bring you, in fact, a glimpse of 'Traveller's Joy'.

Contents

Traveller's Joy

A little voice said to us (only a little voice, but oh so loud and clear) "You say you love this Island with its fields and woods, its chalk downs and little valleys, its streams and multitude of wild flowers. So, go out into the Island, into its highways and byeways, write about it, photograph it, and see if you can communicate to others some of the joy you have found in its wild and lonely places, its stupendous views of land and sea and sky. Go on. Try hard. You never know. You may be lucky"

Main Picture Captions

Along the River Yar

here is no finer time for walking than on a mild day in late October when the sky is blue and the ground is carpeted with fallen leaves in every shade of yellow and brown. On just such a day, when the sky was clear except for a few wisps of cloud, and the sun still had some warmth in it, we started out on a gentle 3 mile circular walk from Langbridge, near Newchurch in the Isle of Wight. (Map Reference 559859).

Langbridge, the 'Long Bridge' over the eastern River Yar at the foot of Newchurch Shute was first mentioned in the 13th century, but the whole area feels older, and there is indeed a rumour of a Roman settlement somewhere in the vicinity, perhaps at Parsonage Farm a little way up the road to the south. From the bridge southwards the road climbs suddenly and steeply up the Shute to the village, where on the brow of the hill the old church with its weatherboarded tower stands guardian over the river valley below.

From Langbridge, and at right angles to the road a public bridleway runs westward parallel with the river and along the old railway line, and this was the way we took. Underfoot the going was level and good apart from a few large puddles left by recent rains, and a gentle sou-westerly breeze was blowing in our faces. Immediately on our left the river flowed smoothly eastwards between steep banks, the water looking peaceful and clean, though weedy. Away to our right, one field width distant, was what appeared to be another stream or ditch with patches of scrub and thorn running parallel to the bridleway. Behind them the ground began to rise from the valley floor, culminating in the mass of Mersley Down a mile away. On

the ridge of the Down the main road from Brading to Newport was visible, a road that has been a highway across the Island for over 2000 years. A few passing motor cars could be seen, but mercifully not heard.

Nothing in fact disturbed the peace of the morning, and we walked on in the warm October sunshine revelling in the tranquillity of the country around us, and thankful for the old dismantled railway track which meant that there were no steep gradients to surmount. After about half a mile a bridge over the river to the left led to another footpath across the fields to Wackland, an interesting farm complex which we were planning to pass later on in our circular route. Soon after passing this footpath, and running parallel to it, was a small tributary to the river, coming down from the high ground near Winford.

On the right across the fields we could now see Haseley Manor and Farm, a large collection of mainly medieval buildings, dominated by the manor house and by a large 16th century barn built in Island stone taken from Quarr Abbey following its dissolution in 1536. Haseley Manor is of course mentioned in Domesday and is one of the oldest inhabited houses in the Isle of Wight.

The original manor house was built in Saxon times, and later in the 12th century it became a Grange of the Abbey of Quarr, the monks producing all their woollen cloth here, and introducing the art of 'fulling' into the Island. The Great Wool Room, built by the monks and containing some 14th century oak roof beams, is still a major part of the house, which from our vantage point near the river, and against the green backdrop of the Downs, looked ageless and indestructible. This

first part of the walk, approximately one mile from Langbridge, came to an end when we reached Horringford, an attractive house and old mill and mill pond, situated on the main Arreton to Sandown Road

into the sun the orderly rows of thousands of fresh green shoots and their shadows made a fascinating picture.

On the far side of the wheat fields we came to a band of woodland and the path went downhill into it. At the bottom was a little trickle of a stream which was in fact the tributary we had previously seen joining the river Yar half a mile or so to the north.

Walking up out of this dip on the other side - and incidentally the only hill to climb on this walk - we were astonished to find a pear tree beside the path. Who on earth could have planted this solitary fruit tree on the edge of this little wood? It was quite an old tree - perhaps it had grown from a pear core carelessly thrown away by a previous user of the footpath. We picked up a few windfalls, but they were not very appetising, being hard and worm eaten.

Wackland, once owned and farmed by the monks of Quarr Abbey.

Newchurch Post Office and Stores, a delightful 300 year old cottage, once the village bakery.

along which we now walked for half a mile, past Hale Manor Farm where a notice board advised us that good coarse fishing was to be had in their extensive lakes. In a cottage on Hale Common near here once lived Elizabeth Wallbridge, 'the Dairyman's Daughter', saintly heroine of 'The Annals of the Poor', by the Reverend Legh Richmond, an early 19th century best seller with sales of over a million copies.

Soon we were able to turn left along a footpath that marked the beginning of the return walk to Newchurch, and we were once more back in the most lovely countryside and could have been miles from civilisation. The broad grassy path we were following led between two huge fields of winter wheat which was already several inches high, and looking southwards

Soon we came to Wackland, a lovely 18th century house with a range of interesting farm buildings. Wackland is interesting both architecturally and historically, and is one of several Island sites where a "Watch" was anciently kept in times of danger. At one time it had belonged to Quarr Abbey, and the fish-pond kept by the monks is still there.

Later, in the 18th century it had belonged to the Thatcher family and became the centre of cock fighting in the Isle of Wight. Just outside the front door is a large circular rose bed which is the site of the cockpit, and old prints show that over the front door was at one time a large porch and a semi-circular room from which the cock fighting was watched. Cock fighting in this area is now remembered by the public house called the Fighting Cocks which is only half a mile from Wackland. This part of the Isle of Wight was famous for its sporting activities in the 18th century, and it was one of the Thatchers who introduced foxes into the Island.

Along Wackland Lane we walked to the Winford to Newchurch road, and were in fact now in the outskirts of this latter attractive village. For all its name Newchurch is very old, and was a thriving community at

From Wackland Lane, looking towards Horringford.

the time of the Norman Conquest. The parish then was huge, stretching from the north coast of the Island to the south, and including both the modern towns of Ryde and Ventnor.

The church itself, dedicated to All Saints, was very prosperous in Norman times and was one of six Island churches given by the Lord of The Island, William Fitz Osbern, to his Abbey of Lyre in Normandy soon after the Conquest. At the beginning of the 15th century the church was purchased from Lyre by the Abbey of Beaulieu in Hampshire, and it was the Beaulieu monks who built the tower of the church in 1420. This tower, which later was weatherboarded, is

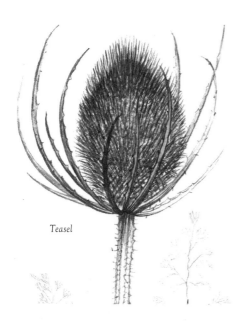

Teasel

9

Haseley Manor with its Venetian window, an 18th century addition to this very old house.

Total Distance Walked: 3 miles.

unique in Island churches, and it can be seen for miles to the north-west, standing as it does at the top of Newchurch Shute above the Yar valley.

The church is beautiful inside, light and bright, clean and airy, and obviously well cared for. It contains some interesting Norman stonework, and memorials to the Dillington family, local Lords of the Manor of Knighton Gorges, and to the Thatchers of Wackland. The village inn, The Pointer, is next door to the church - as it should be - and fulfils its traditional role excellently. Even after a short walk refreshment is always welcome, and the food here is good. In connection with refreshment mention must also be made of Newchurch Post Office and Village Stores, which has a delightful little tea room at the back. Here excellent coffee and tea may be had in the most friendly of surroundings, together with Danish pastries or superb jam doughnuts. Part of this 300 year old cottage was once the village bakery, and it is reputed to be haunted occasionally - and very pleasantly - by the smell of newly baked bread.

From the church a short walk down the very steep Shute, past Parsonage Farm, brought us back to Langbridge and the point where our walk began. This was a gentle stroll of only three miles, and one that can be recommended to those who do not want to walk far and wish to avoid puffing up hills. It can even be shortened to about half the length by turning off the old railway track along the footpath to Wackland, and this would also obviate the half mile walk along a main road. This is also an 'all weather' walk, where the going is never likely to be very heavy, though the sunshine we experienced was a bonus that made it doubly enjoyable.

Did you know ?

1   There was a watermill at Horringford as long ago as the 13th century. It belonged to Quarr Abbey. Records in 1603 say it was 'decayed', but it survived until the 19th century.

2   Teasels are cultivated for use in the textile industry, to raise the nap of woollen cloths such as velour and cashmere.

Walking Points

1   The first part of the walk, from Langbridge to Horringford, is flat and level. Almost one mile, and not normally muddy. In good weather suitable for wheel chairs.

2   The walk may be shortened by taking the footpath over the river to Wackland.

3   Watch your step when crossing the Arreton-Sandown road.

4   The only hill on this walk is approaching Wackland, and this is quite short and not very steep.

5   Both the Pointer Inn and Newchurch Post Office and Stores can be recommended for refreshments. The Inn has a car park, and normally there is no problem parking outside the Post Office. The latter also has a converted barn to let for holidays.

What to look out for

1   Langbridge, the 'Long Bridge' over the river. Did the Romans once build a bridge here?

2   In late October the river bank still has plenty of interesting wild flowers. Predominant were the teasels and a multitude of grasses.

3   Hasely Manor, of Saxon origin. Note the Venetian window in the Manor House, and the huge 16th century barn built of Quarr stone.

4   Wackland House, the 18th century centre of cock fighting.

5   Near Wackland the hill top with its little knot of trees was once the site of an invasion beacon. Watch was kept up here for unwelcome visitors from across the Channel.

6   Between Wackland and Newchurch lie the Works of Wight Crystal Spring Water, a splendid enterprise that finds employment for the handicapped.

7   Note the weather boarded tower of All Saints Church, Newchurch.

8   Inside the church note the unusual gilded lectern in the form of a pelican. Or could it be an eagle?

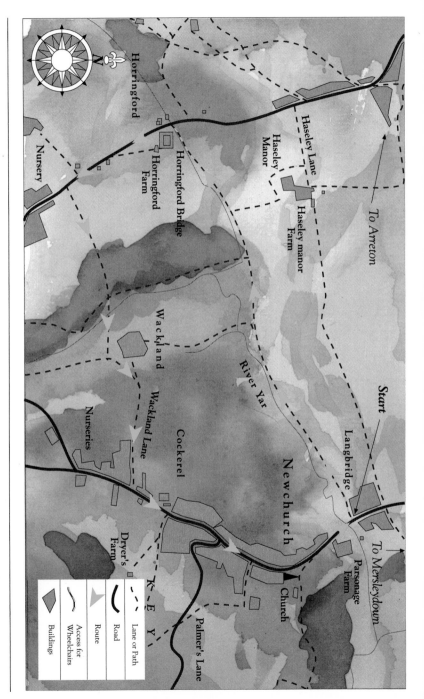

Fishbourne to Binstead

Fishbourne is one of the major ports of entry to the Isle of Wight, Wightlink Ferries running their largest car-carrying ships in from Portsmouth which is 35 minutes distant across the Solent. But though this ferry operation is modern and very busy, Fishbourne, at the mouth of Wootton Creek, is old, as old as the Island itself, and full of history. The Romans are believed to have had a harbour here and to have cultivated oysters in the estuary, though the remains of the oyster beds and fishponds that can still be seen date from a period over 1000 years later when the great Cistercian Abbey of Quarr was built in the 12th century.

If you come off the ferry and turn sharp left you find the Fishbourne Inn, and right opposite the Inn the beginning of a bridle path (Map Ref : 557928) running eastwards parallel with the bank of the Solent and leading to the Abbey. This is the path the monks used when they tended their fishponds and cared for their oysters, and it makes a very pleasant walk indeed, along past the Abbey and on to Binstead, once a remote village, but now on the outskirts of Ryde.

The going is good all the way, though there can be a few muddy patches in the winter after rain, and to be on the safe side boots are advisable. As you leave Fishbourne there are several detached houses on the right with large gardens, and on the left a hedge and trees that allow only the occasional glimpse of the Solent, which is not far away. The path climbs gently for a quarter of a mile, and then as easily descends. Another track crosses it at right angles, and on the left through the trees can be seen the modern red brick Abbey of Quarr, built by French Benedictine monks at the beginning of this century. Is it because of the Abbey that the surroundings here are so peaceful? Whatever the reason one would never suspect that the main Ryde to Newport road is only a matter of a few hundred yards away on the right.

The monks who built the new Abbey left France due to political persecution, and they settled first in the rented old 18th century mansion of Appuldurcombe, near Ventnor. Here they would have stayed and built their Abbey Church had the price been right, but unfortunately when they tried to buy Appuldurcombe they were unable to afford the figure asked, and as an alternative bought an old house and some land that included the ruins of the original Quarr Abbey. It could be argued that this move was ordained by Fate, for the beautiful new Abbey they built is now only a very short distance away from the old one.

As you walk on down the bridleway you come to the farm that occupies the Abbey ruins, a sad reminder of its once great days. The Abbey was founded in 1132 by the Norman Lord of the Island, Baldwin de Redvers, who was trying to take out a little insurance against a possible hostile reception when he died and met his Maker. During his lifetime he had been responsible for the death or maiming of many people, and his conscience was beginning to trouble him.

The Abbey took its name from the limestone quarries in the area which supplied the stone, quarries that had originally been developed by the Romans. Quarr stone became famous, and was used in the construction of Winchester and Chichester Cathedrals, and in Beaulieu and Netley Abbeys. Quarr Abbey too became famous and was by far the largest ecclesiastical foundation in the Isle of Wight. Alas, little of it now

Lesser Celandine

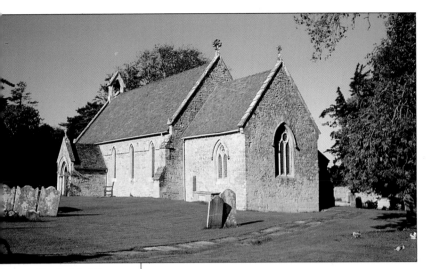

Church of the Holy Cross, Binstead, perhaps originally built for the stone-quarry workers of Quarr.

others that an Abbot of Quarr built it for local people because he found their use of his Abbey Church distracting and irritating. Whatever the date it is indeed very old, though it suffered the inevitable rebuilding in Victorian times when the zeal for turning medieval village churches into mock Gothic temples was at its height. But it contains several interesting features, notably the Rector's stall which is like a miniature Bishop's throne, and indeed for a period after the closure of Quarr Abbey Binstead Church was in the limelight and assumed some of the Abbey's functions and privileges. At this time the Rector was known as the Bishop of Binstead.

The stall itself is heavily and cleverly carved with a representation of Moses sitting on a stone with his arms being held up above his head by his brother Aaron on one side, and by Hur on the other. This little scene is taken from the story in the Bible about

remains, and of the great Abbey Church not a vestige is to be seen.

As you walk past the ruins the path follows the whole length of the Church, proceeding down the middle of what was once the nave and chancel. To the left the Solent can be seen, and to the right a small stream covered in thickets of brambles where the monks maintained a series of fishponds. The Church and most of the other Abbey buildings were demolished in 1539 and the stone sold for building purposes, some of it being used in the construction of Yarmouth Castle.

Once past the old Abbey the path leads through Quarr Wood where a few modern houses have been built, and it is a pleasant level walk to Binstead. The modern village is centred round the main Ryde road, and to the south of it, but here, down near the Solent there is peace and quiet, and when you come out of the wood a little winding lane leads to the old Church of the Holy Cross (Map Ref : 575928).

The exact date of the building of the Church is unknown. Some say it was built for the use of the quarry workers long before the Norman Conquest,

The path that was once the nave of the great Abbey Church of Quarr.

the Israelites on their journey from Egypt to the Promised Land. After their miraculous crossing of the Red Sea, and being fed by manna in the wilderness, they were attacked by the Amalekites, and as long as Moses held up his hands the Israelites prevailed, but as soon as they dropped, the enemy began to win. So that when he grew tired and his hands began to droop, Aaron and Hur held them up. In the Binstead Rector's stall the carved figure of Moses is of course holding up the desk.

Another feature of the Church is that two of the six lancet windows in the north wall are filled with very modern, brightly coloured stained glass, one representing the Virgin Mary and the other John the Baptist. These modern windows were executed by a French studio in Chartres, the traditional home of stained glass, and are as striking as any in the Island.

After passing the church the path is narrower, and in fact continues for just over a quarter of a mile, crossing the golf links, until it converges with the main road at the Golf Club House, but before reaching this point walkers can turn left over a little stream and go down to the beach. Near this spot is Binstead Hard, where traditionally Binstead stone was exported to the mainland, and this quiet spot with a few boats moored off-

Dormouse, berries and catkins

shore and the gentle lapping of the water on the shingle really marks the halfway point in the walk, for here one must turn for home.

The route back is almost the same as the route out, except for one deviation in Quarr wood along a slightly muddy footpath. Here on either side is a tangled mass of vegetation where large depressions in the ground can be seen. These are the old stone pits

All that remains of the original Abbey of Quarr.

where the limestone was quarried, and at one time the area rang to the sound of hammers and chisels, to the noise of great blocks of stone being moved, and to the hum of many men's voices. But now all is quiet, the woods are still and silent, and the Binstead quarries are dead.

On the way back past the Abbey ruins spare a thought as you walk the length of the vanished church for the many people buried there whose graves have been lost. Baldwin de Redvers himself, the founder, lies somewhere under this bridleway, and other Norman Lords of the Island and their ladies. And an even more illustrious person, the Princess Cecily, daughter of King Edward IV of England, who was buried here in

The Rector's stall, with Moses supporting the desk.

Princess's resting place should go unnoticed, and was prepared to mount a suitable memorial stone if the grave could be found.

So she sent a well known Island architect, the elderly but irascible Percy Goddard Stone, to see what he could discover. On the site he met some of the French monks who were preparing to build the new Abbey, but unfortunately they knew no English and he could not speak French, so that very soon they were at cross purposes and the monks were unable to understand his quest for the grave of a woman. In fact they got quite the wrong idea, and ultimately one of them, summoning up the few English words at his command, said rather brusquely "We are monks, and there are definitely no women here!"

As you pass the new Abbey you may be lucky enough to see some of the monks walking back to the Abbey from their work in the fields, or to hear the Abbey bell calling them to one of the many daily services, to certain of which the public are welcome. In such peaceful surroundings this experience has a tremendously calming effect, and is a powerful and soothing antidote to the stress and noise of everyday life. Strolling on down the track to Fishbourne you will feel refreshed, for this walk is as good for the spirit as it is for the body.

1507 only a few years before the Abbey was closed, and whose grave, along with the others, has left no trace.

An amusing story is told of one attempt to find the grave of this royal Princess. Queen Victoria, when she came to live in the Island, felt it was wrong that the

Total Distance Walked : 3.25 miles

Did you know ?

1   The old Abbey of Quarr was closed down by Henry VIII in 1536.

2   The new Quarr Abbey was built in 1908.

3   Underneath the site of the old Abbey Church is the grave of a Royal Princess, a daughter of Edward IV, Princess Cecily. Also the grave of Baldwin de Redvers, founder of the Abbey.

Walking Points

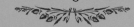

1 Cars may be parked in Fishbourne Lane, or if you are visiting the Fishbourne Inn (recommended), in their car park.

2 The going generally is good, but after heavy rain there may be muddy patches, and boots are recommended.

3 As you pass the Abbey ruins the track runs down what was the centre of the nave of the great Abbey Church.

4 After passing Binstead Church turn left along the footpath to Binstead Hard. Alternatively, carry straight on for another 1/4 mile or so across the golf links, but then turn back.

5 The footpath through Quarr Wood is sometimes muddy.

6 Parts of the walk are suitable for wheel chairs, notably between Binstead Church and the Abbey ruins.

7 Finish at the Fishbourne Inn, frequently voted the Island's best pub. The food here is excellent.

What to look out for

1 The modern and imposing Quarr Abbey on the left. The public are welcomed to some of the services.

2 The old Abbey ruins, also on the left. On the right the remains of one of the monks' fish stews, or ponds.

3 Visit the Church of the Holy Cross at Binstead, and note particularly the heavily carved Rector's stall, and the two modern stained glass windows.

4 As you enter the church look up to the left, and note the beautiful praying head.

5 In the churchyard note the double headstone to Thomas Sivell and his wife. Thomas was a fisherman, but was shot by the Excisemen who thought he was a smuggler.

6 Binstead Hard, near the end of the footpath to the beach, was the point from which Quarr stone was exported to the mainland.

7 On either side of the footpath through Quarr Wood note depressions in the ground which are all that remain of the old quarries.

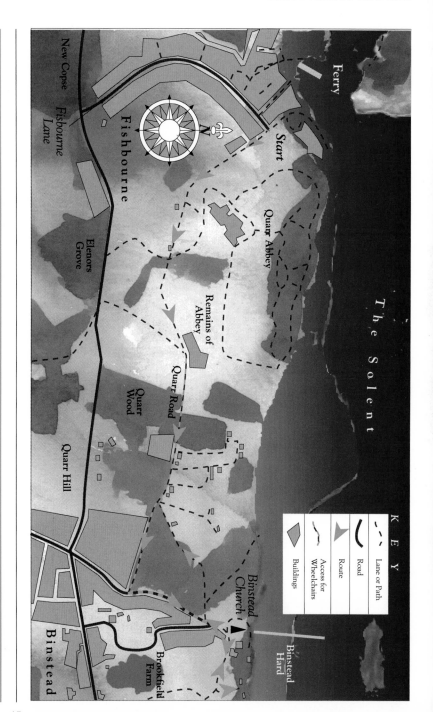

A Downsway Walk

The Downs Road is one of the Isle of Wight's oldest and most fascinating roads. It runs for about 5 miles from east to west along the top of the chalk ridge which is the backbone of the Island. Its course is more or less straight, with varying gradients, from Downend in the west to Brading in the east, and on its way it affords some of the most spectacular views, both to the north and the south. Here you are really on top of the world, and it does not require a great stretch of the imagination to conjure up pictures of the wildness and beauty of the area before its peace was spoiled by the motor car.

By modern standards there is not a lot of traffic on the Downs Road, though what there is is noisy. But once off the road, on either side, the peace and quiet is blissful, and you are soon immersed in the sort of glorious domestic scenery with which the Isle of Wight abounds, and it would not be surprising if on your way you met travellers of another age who were, say, journeying from the Roman Villa of Combley at Downend to the great natural harbour of Brading Haven, perhaps calling at the other Roman Villa at Morton on the way.

Today my wife and I decided on a short circular walk of about 4 miles, starting from a spot on the Downs Road where there is a small car park, (Map Ref : 591870) and taking one of the many public footpaths to the north of the road. Fortunately, footpaths in the Isle of Wight are very well signposted, so that it is easy to plan such a walk on the map and then go out and enjoy yourselves. Today the sky was blue with a few scudding clouds, and up on the top there was an easterly breeze blowing of about force 3. As we arrived at the little car park we could see the whole sweep of Sandown Bay away to the south, and to the north the town of Ryde and the Solent 3 to 4 miles distant, though the town was far enough away to be merely a pleasant prospect without obtruding on the peacefulness of the scene. Further north, mistily, we could see the mainland of England.

Some Conservation Volunteers were getting out of a blue van in the car park and preparing to move off down the path to the south armed with axes and other tools. We crossed the road however and went through a five barred gate under a signpost pointing north with the message "Public Footpath No.30 to Nunwell Farm" and another, more recent sign, that just said 'Downsway Walk', with an arrow.

Once through the gate the panorama before us, as we walked steadily downhill, was breathtaking. In front of us were miles of rolling countryside, fields, farms, and woods, and to the left on a hilltop almost exactly a mile away gleamed the Ashey sea-mark, a white triangular stone pillar erected in 1735 to guide mariners who were negotiating the waters of the Foreland off Bembridge.

The path we were on soon forked, the left hand plunging steeply downhill to join another track below which led directly to Nunwell Farm, but we kept straight on and very soon turned to the right along the brow of the Down until halted by a wire fence. On the other side of this was a large and very old disused chalk pit. Here, hundreds of years ago, men had gouged chalk out of the hillside and spread it on their farms to sweeten the land, but now it was no longer a scar, for Nature had reclaimed it, vegetation had grown and it was full of trees. We scrambled down the

Meadow Vetchling flower

hill by the side of the pit to join a bridleway below which took us, on level ground, through a long narrow belt of woodland known as Nunwell Hanging Wood, but on some maps referred to as Kelly's Copse.

Dappled sunshine in Nunwell Hanging Wood.

This path, running straight through the wood, was exceedingly pretty, many of the trees being magnificent beeches of considerable age, and the effect of the dappled sunshine on the path was very pleasing. Many of the trees had suffered in the winter gales and had to be sawn up to clear the path, but already the devastation caused by their falling was effectively covered by new vegetation.

A very little way along this path we came to a signpost and another path shooting off to the left. This one led alongside a wood noted for its rookery and culminating in the West Lodge to Nunwell Park and House, one of the Island's most beautiful and celebrated country estates. We remembered this path particularly having once walked it in the winter, in freezing rain, but having been delighted to watch the antics of about a dozen long-tailed tits who were quite oblivious to the weather.

Nunwell's fame derives from it having been the home for over 800 years of the Oglander family, an astonishing record of ownership. The most famous member of the family was Sir John Oglander who was born in 1585, for it is to him that we owe almost all our knowledge of life in the Island during the first three decades of the 17th century. Sir John was not exactly a diarist but he wrote extensively about his life and times, and his writings and scribblings have survived, to the delight and edification of present day historians.

As we proceeded along this path we passed the end of a wide avenue of majestic limes stretching to the north and leading to Nunwell House itself, which could be glimpsed occasionally through the trees. The path we were on did in fact mark the southernmost boundary of the Nunwell estate, and in due course we turned sharp left along the eastern boundary, the original path continuing on until ultimately reaching the little town of Brading, itself one of the most historic places in the Isle of Wight. This eastern boundary path, along the edge of a field of ripening corn, gave us to our right a charming glimpse of Brading church nestling among trees, and led to a little side road called Coach Lane. A few yards along this was East Lodge, the main entrance to Nunwell, and immediately past the Lodge was a stile on the left which brought us face to face with another large field of corn. Across this field and through the middle of the waist high wheat the path plunged, straight across to the far side, being very narrow and difficult to see as the wheat on each side was less than a foot apart. In the middle of the field we got the very novel impression of wading waist deep through a golden sea, and a little French poem by Guy de Maupassant came to mind -

"Les blés, les blés, les puissants blés
Ondulent sous le vent... "

(The corn, the corn, the powerful corn
Undulates in the breeze...)

We have all seen the way a ripple goes across a cornfield when the wind blows, but to use the word "puissant", which means powerful, to describe the strength of the corn is intriguing. "Puissant" is an interesting word which even found its way into the English language in the days when the French influence was still very strong in this country. Shakespeare used it frequently in describing the power of princes - for instance, he refers to King Henry V as "my thrice-puissant liege" - so that to find it used to describe standing corn is curious and delightful. I have even seen it on a crane in Cherbourg harbour, which was labelled as being of "puissance 40 tonnes". It is truly a powerful word, being capable of so many shades of meaning.

The next field we crossed was a complete contrast, being grassy and containing a herd of Friesian cows. To our right were the sprawling buildings of New Farm, and in the field various hummocks covering the remains of previous buildings, which may even have been built by the great Sir John himself about 350 years ago. Ahead lay Nunwell Farm, a conglomerate of buildings of various materials including clunch, a local product of compressed chalk blocks, perfectly satisfactory for walls, but not strong enough for corners, so that clunch buildings almost invariably have brick quoins.

Through the waist high wheat.

Our way lay through the farmyard and past a barn containing hay, the exposed part of which was covered with a black tarpaulin held down by the largest collection of old motor tyres we had seen for a long time. We were now well on our way to completing the circular tour we had undertaken, and the ground steadily rose as we faced the ascent back to the top of the Downs. One last steep pull of a few hundred yards and we were back at the gate we had first entered. We were both glad to sit down for a rest in the car and just watch the countryside spread out below us to the south, with one or two big ships way out in the Channel.

Beech trees in Kelly's Copse.

been uncovered, but some of the mosaic floors are very fine, and amazingly well preserved. The villa is sited on a hillside facing east in what must have been a truly magnificent position, for in the days when it was built, nearly 2000 years ago, the sea came up to the bottom of the hill, only a few hundred yards from their front door.

After spending an hour or two in the Roman Villa it was time to visit another favourite haunt only just round the corner, this being Morton Manor which is also open to the public. Morton Manor is a very old house with extensive grounds, and even has its own vineyard which produces a series of fine white and rosé wines. But the true glory of Morton lies in its gardens which are superb; sweeping lawns, a variety of beautiful trees and herbaceous borders full of glorious colour. Time spent in these serene and restful surroundings is time well spent, and will soothe and calm anyone suffering from the pressures of living under stress from traffic noise, telephones, or pollution of any other kind.

As we sat and sipped our Earl Grey tea under the shade of a beautiful old lime tree, we reflected on our good fortune in being able to enjoy the Downs, the fields of ripening corn, the Roman Villa, and the haven of these tranquil gardens.

As it was lunch time we motored the mile or so into the outskirts of Brading to visit a favourite pub, the Anglers Inn at Yarbridge, where the beer is always at just the right temperature, and food is well above the standard one expects to find in a pub. Suitably refreshed, it was then only half a mile or so to the Roman Villa at Morton which was discovered and excavated in 1880, and which is open to the public and always worth a visit. This is a large complex of house and farm buildings, not all of which have yet

Total Distance
Walked : 4 miles

Did you know ?

1   Nunwell House was occupied by one family, the Oglanders, for over 800 years.

2   Sir John Oglander (1585-1655) is our principal source of information on life in the Isle of Wight at that time.

3   Charles I stayed at Nunwell in 1647.

4   Peace and tranquillity are to be found in the gardens of Morton Manor.

Walking Points

1   There is a small car park at Map Reference 591870.

2   Cross the road · watch the traffic · and footpath 30 is almost opposite.

3   Follow the path round the wire fence to the right, and down the hillside by the disused chalk pit. The bridleway is then easy to follow.

4   The public footpath from Coach Lane to Nunwell Farm goes directly across the fields which may be growing crops, but the footpath should still be clearly seen.

5   The climb back up to the Downs Road is short but steep.

6   This is an undulating walk with frequent changes in terrain.

What to look out for

1   Magnificent views over Sandown Bay to the south, and north-wards to Ryde and the Solent.

2   The Ashey Seamark to the west.

3   The disused chalk pit is medieval, but nature has reclaimed it.

4   Note the attractive Nunwell Hanging Wood, or Kelly's Copse.

5   Glimpses of Nunwell House through the trees.

6   Picturesque view of Brading Church across the cornfield.

7   Notice the clunch built barn with brick quoins at Nunwell Farm.

8   Brading Roman Villa is well worth a visit, and so is Morton Manor.

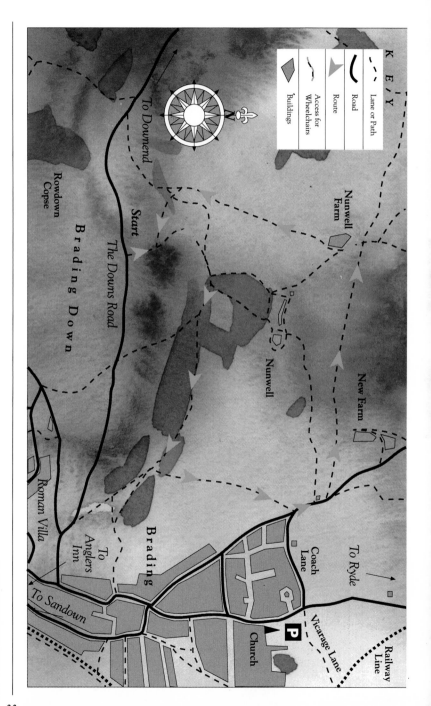

Monks and Nuns

The 'Blacksmith's Arms' is a very old country inn which has welcomed travellers, as well as blacksmiths, for centuries. It lies on the road from Carisbrooke to Calbourne in the Isle of Wight, and roughly midway between the two villages. The road is known locally as the Middle Road for it runs across the Island from Newport to the West Wight, with another parallel road a mile or two to the north (the Newport to Yarmouth road), and a somewhat similar one to the south, the Military Road, which was built in the 19th century for the rapid movement of troops and guns at a time when the Isle of wight was threatened by Napoleon.

The 'Blacksmith's Arms' makes a very good starting off point for a particularly interesting walk along old bridleways and ancient highways, and - let it be said - it is perhaps equally attractive as the finishing point. With this in mind the car may be left in the pub car park, though alternatively there is a good bus service from Newport with a bus stop immediately outside the pub.

From this starting off point (Map Ref : 465879) it is possible to carry out many circular walks of varying lengths, from about 1.5 miles up to as many miles as there are hours of daylight, but the one about to be described is a modest three miles long though it involves a steepish climb to begin with to get up on to the Downs. One of the glories of walking in the Isle of Wight is that you are never very far away from the chalk Downs, which are themselves glorious and well worth the pull to get up to the top.

Almost immediately opposite the pub car park is an old bridleway. Cross the road carefully, for though there is not a lot of traffic along the Middle Road, what there is whistles along. Having crossed however you are soon away from civilisation. The bridleway is a sunken track between trees, the surface is good for walking, but it rises steadily and steeply. Sunken tracks very often suggest an old boundary, but this one is curious in that for several hundred yards there is another sunken track running alongside it to the right. Could it be perhaps that the bank of earth between the two was in this case the boundary?

Near the top the covering of trees comes to an end, and through a small gate the path leads into a cornfield. Round the edge of this to the right the path goes, the ground still rising, and underfoot the route becomes more chalky with many large stones and flints. As you near the brow of the hill and look over the low hedge to the right the views become more and more breathtaking - though perhaps it is just the climb that takes your breath away! Immediately on the other side of the hedge the ground is lower, and it could be that the original old bridleway lies here, and that the path we are on is more recent.

But the views to the north and north west are truly worth seeing. To the north the eye is taken along the line of a straight lane - Betty Haunt Lane - towards the dark edge of Parkhurst Forest a few miles away, with the Solent beyond. Betty, incidentally, is said to have been a smuggler's daughter who used her feminine wiles to distract the Excise men when a cargo was being run. Unfortunately for her she fell in love with one of the customs officials and betrayed her smuggling associates, many of whom were caught and punished. Some escaped however and caught poor Betty, and her body was found in the lane that now

Field Bindweed

bears her name. To the north west you see a patchwork quilt of fields and woods, with here and there an isolated farm, Great Park, Upper Watchingwell, and others, and beyond them the spread of Newtown harbour, its creeks and inlets for all the world like the outstretched fingers of a hand. In Clamerkin Lake, the most easterly inlet, several yachts could be seen at anchor, microscopic white dots against the blue of the distance.

A large tortoiseshell butterfly feeds on blackberry flowers.

Once on the top of the Downs the ground levels off, and in the corner of the cornfield the path turns sharp left to meet another, and possibly even older, trackway, wide and flat, which runs all the way from Carisbrooke in a south-westerly direction to Brighstone Forest, where in a maze of ancient highways and lost villages you can take your pick and travel north, south, east, or west. But that is a much longer walk. At the point where we met this very ancient highway, only about half a mile from our starting point, there was once an Anglo-Saxon burial ground, but that was over 1000 years ago, and now there is only solitude. We took the old highway towards Brighstone for nearly another mile, following the ridge of the Downs, surrounded by glorious country, and with only the sounds of nature as accompaniment. Along this highway, which is bordered on the right by a hedge, can be found in autumn the best blackberries in the Isle of Wight.

At the end of this exhilarating stretch, on the roof of the Island, with Bowcombe Wood away down to the left, and Monkham Copse to the right, you come to a point where five tracks meet (Map Ref: 456860). One of these goes back north-east to Bowcombe Wood,

before swinging east down into Bowcombe, one goes south-east and soon forks, the left fork going east past a disused chalk pit and then down to cross the Bowcombe Road near Idlecombe. The right Fork heads off in a southerly direction to Rowborough Farm. The next one is a continuation of the ancient highway. we were on and carries on through Brighstone Forest to its junction with the network of tracks mentioned above, at Map Ref.434843. But we were due to take the fourth one, leading almost due north, to bring us back to the Blacksmith's Arms (1.75 miles).

This track goes down through Monkham Copse for about half a mile, not a steep descent, but a wide winding path through the woods which had been cleared on either side of the track. In the middle ages it was quite common to cut woodland back on either side of a highway, to lessen the danger of being attacked by robbers, though I doubt whether this was the reason on this particular track. The practice is said to have been started by Edward I when he was fighting the Welsh. He was ambushed so many times that in self defence he cleared the woodland a full bowshot on either side of the road.

The derivation of the name 'Monkham' is simple, it means 'belonging to the monks'. But which monks?

.... found ourselves passing through the greatest profusion of wild flowers.

Could it be the monks of Quarr Abbey? They held land and farms in all parts of the Island, so that conceivably it could have been theirs. But perhaps a stronger possibility is that the monks were from Hyde Abbey in Winchester, for Monkham was for many centuries a part of the manor of Swainston in Calbourne, and Swainston House was the summer palace of the Bishops of Winchester who were also Abbots of Hyde. Swainston Manor House, now an Hotel, is only about a mile from Monkham Copse and is one of the most historically interesting sites in the Isle of Wight.

But there is another, very intriguing, point. Monkham Copse is on the west facing slope of Bowcombe Down and immediately opposite it the ground rises sharply to another Down - Apes Down. This name is a contraction of Abbess's Down, and records show that in the year 1250 Alice the Abbess of Wilton bought some land here. So it looks as though at one time the little valley separating these two Downs was also separating land belonging to the nuns of Wilton from land owned by the monks of Hyde. Maybe there is no connection between the two, but what a fascinating thought! However, after that digression we continued on down the hill, and suddenly our progress became very slow indeed for we found ourselves passing through the greatest profusion of wild flowers we have ever seen and we just had to stop and look at them and photograph them. Also it was around noon on a hot summers day and we were very warm. We were walking north, the sun on our backs and our shadows straight before us, very short and dark. But any discomfort we felt was forgotten at the sight of the flowers, for there was such a kaleidoscope of colour, and even though, having lived in the Isle of Wight for many years we were used to seeing wild flowers in the hedgerows and verges, the display we saw here in Monkhams Copse caused us both to exclaim.

There were great clumps of rosebay willow herb on the edges of the wood shining out against the dark green of the trees, and patches of tall spear-thistles with their large purple flowers. There were many other thistles, particularly lower down in the bottom of the valley between the two Downs which was a grassy area. There were also teasels, marjoram, hemp agrimony, and the tall Great Mullein or Aaron's Rod, though this was beginning to seed.

On the verges of the track there were scabious, patches of toadflax and self heal, the latter being a plant renowned in medieval times for its curative properties, and the butterflies were having a field day. We saw many large whites, both male and female, large tortoiseshells and small skippers. Partridges were popping in and out of the woods, but apart from these and a few blue tits we saw little bird life - perhaps it was too hot in the noonday sun, or perhaps we were not observant enough. When we reached the bottom of Monkham Wood a gate and stile led out into the wide grassy valley running from the Downs in a northeasterly direction. Obviously the valley had once carried a stream of some size, and the Ordnance Survey map does show a stream wandering across country northwards until it becomes the Clamerkin Brook emptying into Clamerkin Lake of Newtown harbour, where for centuries oysters have been cultivated. The name Clamerkin is the last remaining relic of the old Norman family of Clamorgan or Glamorgan who were powerful in the Island in the 12th and 13th centuries.

We crossed this valley to another stile leading on to Rowridge Lane, a narrow private road running along the side of Apes Down from the Carisbrooke to Calbourne Road up to the TV Station on the top of Rowridge to the south. Along this lane we went, down the valley for three quarters of a mile, marvelling at the wealth of flowers in the hedgerows on either hand, harebells and honeysuckle, old man's beard, which is perhaps better known as Travellers Joy, bilberries (also known in the south as whortleberries or hurt) cobnut trees, oak and ash, everything very lush and in

Ox-eye Daisy and
Common Dog Violet

An old granary on staddle stones in Rowridge Lane.

incredible profusion. The lane followed the edge of the valley to the north-east, and it *was* an edge, for on the other side of the hedge there was almost a sheer drop of 100 feet or so. Here, as on the Monkham side of the valley, there had been no crop spraying, and the array of wild flowers and their many colours were glorious to behold. To the left of the lane the ground rose steeply to Apes Down and was wooded, although there were a couple of steep fields of cabbages. Did the nuns from Wilton Abbey grow cabbages, we wondered?

There were also signs here and there of water having cascaded off the Down and across the road bringing lumps of chalk with it. A beautiful, unspoilt country lane, giving us a glimpse of what this incredible Island could be like if crop spraying and verge cutting could be controlled. Obviously farmers have to make a profit, but in fact they seem to produce too much and create mountains of surplus grain, etc. We do not seem to be able to control our economy very efficiently, and the environment suffers as a consequence.

As we went down Rowridge Lane the views across the valley to our right were beautiful. We looked across to Monkham Copse and Bowcombe Down where we had been walking only an hour or so before, and actually spotted trees on the skyline that we had passed. Down the lane we came to Apesdown Farm Cottage which had a lovely cottage garden full of

bloom, and with more wild flowers in the hedgerows outside, a peaceful and idyllic spot. At the bottom of the lane we came to Rowridge House on the right, a large old house presumably once a farmhouse for on the left of the lane was an old brick built granary in a very dilapidated state. The bricks were laid in English bond - alternate rows of headers and stretchers - and the building was mounted on staddle stones to keep out the rats, but a bygone farmer had provided a flight of stone steps up to a door, now broken, so that the rats could get in after all!

This last leg of the walk was the least pleasant because it was on the main road and the road surface was very hot from have been in the sun all morning, but it was not much more that half a mile and traffic was not troublesome. The saloon bar of the 400 year old Blacksmith's Arms was cool, and the refreshment dispensed by the landlord was most welcome. As we sat in the pub's dining room and looked out to the north over the scenery that we had so recently seen from the top of the Down we were at peace with the world.

Total Distance Walked : 3 miles.

Did you know ?

1   The Ancient Highway starts in Carisbrooke and runs all the way to Brighstone Forest, where it joins another great east to west highway reaching to the Needles. It skirts Gallibury Fields and an area dotted with Tumuli and the sites of lost villages. The past comes to meet you as you travel this road.

2   When you join the ancient highway at Map Reference 461872 you are in a timeless world. You can see ghosts up here - pedlars, tinkers, wandering minstrels. Also other modern walkers!

What to look out for

1   The sunken bridleway from the Blacksmiths Arms up on to the Down has another sunken track running parallel to it. Was the ridge in between them a boundary wall?

2   When you reach the top just look at the views to the north and west with the Solent in the distance.

3   The Anglo-Saxon Burial Ground is marked on the Ordnance Survey as a Tumulus.

4   Along the Highway in autumn you will find the biggest and juiciest blackberries in the Island.

5   The track down through Monkhams Copse will present you with a profusion of wild flowers, and I defy you not to slow down. We saw scabious, marjoram, hemp agrimony, great mullein, toad flax, self heal, rosebay willow herb, and many others. A riot of colour. Also tortoiseshell butterflies and Skippers and large and small whites. Monkhams Copse was alive.

5   In Rowridge Land more wild flowers, and a glory of Travellers Joy.

6   Notice the old granary at Rowridge House.

Walking Points

1   The Blacksmiths Arms is on the main road and bus route from Newport to Calbourne and Freshwater.

2   It is a steepish climb from the main road up on to the Down.

3   Ignore the fork to the left shortly after leaving the road. (Reserve this for another day).

4   Five bridleways meet at Map Reference 455860. Turn sharp right here down through Monkhams Copse.

5   At the bottom of the Copse go through he gate and cross the field to Rowridge Lane.

6   The surface of Rowridge Lane, and of course the main road, are suitable for wheel chairs · but do please watch it. The main road is a busy one, so that great care is needed. And though Rowridge Lane carries negligible traffic, it is steep in places.

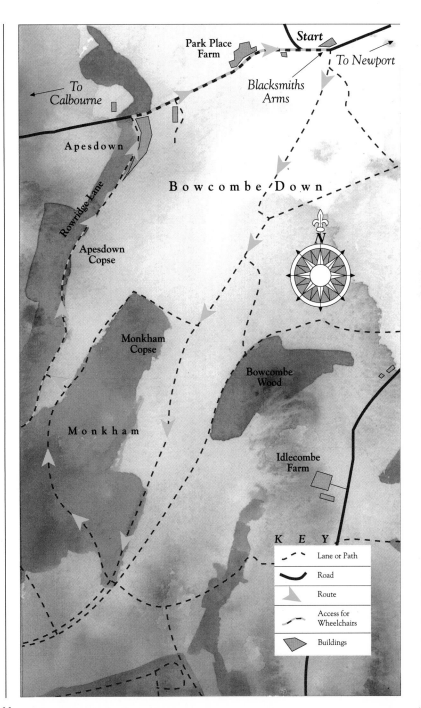

A Walk into the Past

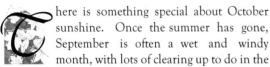

There is something special about October sunshine. Once the summer has gone, September is often a wet and windy month, with lots of clearing up to do in the garden, and outlook at this time generally is pretty dismal, with the excitement of Christmas still a long way away. And then suddenly, early in October, you get a most perfect day, a dog-day perhaps, when the sky is blue and the sun is warm without being too hot, and there is a lovely mellow light that softens all the colours of the turning leaves, producing a most harmonious and relaxing sheen to the countryside. And it is then more than good to be out walking.

It was on just such an October day that we decided on a modest walk of about three miles starting at Havenstreet (Map Reference 563905), proceeding generally in a southerly direction, and making our way ultimately to Combley Farm. For the sake of interest we followed a circular route, but it is also a very pleasant walk just to go straight to Combley and back, and if you do this it cuts about half a mile off the trip.

The village of Havenstreet is a most unusual and interesting place, straggling along for about three quarters of a mile on both sides of the road, with beautiful open country on either side. It is very old, and indeed it is believed that the road passing through the village was originally Roman, though this has never been proved. However, a look at the Ordnance Survey Map discloses some strange and intriguing facts, and makes it possible to offer a guess as to where the road came from and where it was going to. The road runs straight through the village from north-east to south-west, and it is possible without using too much imagination to follow its further course at both

ends. To the north-east its line crosses the fields to join Newnham Road in Binstead, and then continuing in a straight line down to the old stone quarries. At the other, south-westerly end, and just outside the village, the road becomes public bridleway No.18 which marches off across country in a sou-westerly direction straight to Combley Farm.

Now, the significance of all this is that just past Combley Farm is the site of a Roman Villa, and at least part of the Villa was built of stone. So it looks as though this ancient track could have been laid down by the Romans in the first century A.D. specifically to carry the necessary stone from the quarries to the site where they had chosen to build their house. This is an intriguing possibility worthy of further investigation.

Bridleway No.18 actually begins near Havenstreet Station (Map Reference 554897). It is quite a wide gravelly track, and it is possible to leave the car here where the track starts. It runs parallel to and along the edge of Walkers Hill Copse and is extremely pretty with the dappled sunshine through the trees. About a quarter of a mile in from the road there is a large clearing where a tree-felling and log stacking operation has been carried out, and here the track forks to the left. No.18 carries straight on but as we had decided to make a circular journey of it we took the left fork which passes right through the Copse.

Another quarter of a mile further on a wooden bridge crosses Deadmans Brook, a stream that once had considerably more water in it than it has to-day, and no doubt received its rather sinister name from a dead man having been found in it. But if he was drowned it must have been a long time ago. After crossing the

WARNING
Since this book was published, it has been brought to the author's attention that there is NO PUBLIC RIGHT OF WAY from the left hand fork about a quarter of a mile from the start of the walk described and leading across Dead Man's Brook and through Duxmore Farm. Readers should not therefore take this route, but should remain on BRIDLEWAY No. 18 which leads to Combley Farm and is a public right of way.

Spear Thistle

stream the track leaves Walkers Hill Copse and comes out into the open before running along the east side of Hoglease Copse, and then across the fields in a southerly direction towards the high ground of Mersley Down. Although the Downs here are not particularly high, only 135 metres (about 400 feet) running from east to west they dominate the skyline, and all along the slope near the top can be seen the scars of old chalk pits where for centuries man has dug the chalk to put on his land. Indeed, the track we were on actually terminates in one such pit, one that looks as though it could even be still in use.

But before we reached this pit a change of course was necessary. At Map Reference 552878 another track goes off at right angles eastwards to Duxmore Farm, the roof of which could be seen nestling in a clump of trees only 300 yards away But our way lay in the opposite direction, to the west, on a footpath across the fields. The whole of this area around Duxmore, and Little Duxmore which is further to the east, has a very old feel to it, and as well as a Roman presence it is believed to have been the scene of a particularly bloody battle between the Jutes and the Saxons when the latter conquered the Isle of Wight in A.D.686. But now it is peaceful and still, and we paused at this point for a few moments to savour the beauty of the countryside around us and the tranquillity of this pastoral scene. We sat on a low bank by the side of the track in the sunshine and drank a welcome

The arrow-straight bridleway No. 18. Could it have been built by the Romans?

cup of coffee from our flask. This immediately attracted the attention of a beautiful shire horse and foal, and two whiter-than-white Angora goats in the field behind us, who were all most interested in the possibility of there being something in it for them. While my wife took a few photographs I wandered along the hedgerow picking blackberries.

Away on the high ground to the east about a mile and a half distant we could see the sea mark on Ashey Down, a white obelisk erected in 1735 to guide sailors off the east coast of the Island. Ahead of us to the west, and only about half a mile away, were the trees surrounding Combley Farm, and beyond that the high ground leading up to Downend, on the eastern slope of which is the site of Combley Roman Villa. On the way to the farm we walked along the edge of a large field already a brilliant green colour from a crop of winter wheat that was 3-4 inches high, and through the hedge we could see the ploughman in the next

Modern husbandry at work; a stack of logs in a woodland clearing.

field, followed by hundreds of seagulls. The soil was chocolate brown in colour and looked very rich. Soon we came to a gate from which we could look down a slope to Combley Farm, a truly idyllic spot.

Deadmans Brook flows through Combley, and indeed the springs that feed it and are its source rise on the hillside not far away. These springs were of course the water supply for the Roman Villa and must have been a major influence in its siting here. Looking down on the tree lined stream in this little valley, protected from the prevailing westerly and southerly winds, it is easy to see why the Romans chose such a spot. Who was the Roman who built a house here? He must have been a man of substance, and as the Combley Villa was built early on in the Occupation he was no doubt a soldier, and a fairly high ranking one at that. Is it conceivable that perhaps it was Vespasian himself, the commander of the Second Legion that first occupied the Island in A.D.43? Vespasian is known to have been a good man, of equable temperament, and such a one as might have appreciated the peace and quiet provided by this beautiful countryside. he became Emperor of Rome in A.D.69 and died ten years later.

Meanwhile, with our feet firmly planted on the 20th century ground we walked down to Combley farm, through the farm yard, and proceeded along bridleway 18 back towards Havenstreet. For the first half mile that track is out in the open, running parallel to Deadmans Brook, and then it passes into Hoglease Copse. After one mile a footpath (No.93) forks off to the left across the fields to Guildford Farm, and shortly after that we reached the clearing and the pile of logs where we branched off to the left on the way out, and from here we could see in the distance, far down the track through the tunnel of trees, our parked car.

This was an interesting and not too difficult walk, the total distance being about 3.5 miles. Bridleway 18 is a good and solid, road-like track, a little stony in places, which makes it rather hard on the feet, and with a few potholes which fill with water after rain. But generally it is so firm and well drained that one wonders if it has Roman foundations. Where it passes through open country the hedgerow on its western side is thick and lush, containing a wide variety of shrubs and small trees. To try and give a date to the age of this hedge we carried out the standard sampling of a thirty yard length of hedge, and counted at least ten different species. Applying then the formula given by David Streeter and Rosamund Richardson in their book "Discovering hedgerows" which is -

Age of hedge = No. of species in 30 yards x 110 + 30 years we get a total of 1130 years, which takes us back to A.D.860. We make no claim that our sampling was accurate, and indeed a skilled botanist might well have discovered more species, but any hedge over a thousand years old is entitled to respect.

Incidentally, 'Discovering Hedgerows' is much to be recommended to all who love the countryside. It is based on a B.B.C. television series first broadcast in 1982, and is full of fascinating information.

The principal species seen in this long hedgerow include blackthorn, quickthorn, oak, ash, hazel, elder, holly, dogwood, and of course roses and brambles. Dogwood is a most interesting shrub with a long history, and is also known as the 'dog tree' or 'dogberry' since its black fruit is inedible and not even fit for dogs. From medieval times butchers have used skewers or 'dogs' made from the hard white wood of this shrub, and the black berries have been used as a source of lamp oil. Shakespeare knew the plant and named one of the comic rural characters in Much Ado About Nothing, 'Dogberry'. In autumn the green dogwood leaves gradually turn red, in shades varying from a bright orange-red to a very deep purple. There were many varieties of berries in this hedge, including hawthorn, rose, spindle, and black bryony. Spindle berries are a delicate shade of red and are

Combley Farm and pond; remote and enchanting.

The only discordant noet in an otherwise blissfully peaceful rural scene was, for a short time in the early stages of the walk, the noise made by two small aircraft very high up and continually diving and climbing with their engines droning and screaming away. When we came out into the open near Hoglease Copse we could just see them, silver specks against the deep blue sky, twisting and turning, looping and rolling, but polluting the air with their hideous noise. We know that young men have to learn to fly, and indeed we remember with gratitude that in 1940 the free world was saved by such young men, but do they have to practice over the land where hundreds of people have to put up with their noise? Only a few miles further on they would have been over the open sea and out of earshot. This is perhaps a carping criticism, though in our world to-day noise is a principal source of pollution.

However, the sun continued to shine just as brightly after they had gone, and for the remainder of our walk we were accompanied only by normal country sounds and soon forgot the temporary disturbance. After the walk was over we drove the half mile or so into Havenstreet village to the White Hart Inn. It is not by accident that our walks are usually planned to terminate within reasonable reach of some village pub, and we can confidently recommend the White Hart. It is a friendly place where the food is as good as any in the Island, and better than most.

unusual in shape, being four-lobed, and from above looking more like flowers than berries. The bright red berries of the black bryony are truly fantastic, both in quantity and in richness of colour. They are poisonous and both birds and animals shun them. The plant was well known in the middle ages, a poultice of the berries being a cure for chilblains, and also being used to treat freckles, sunburn, black eyes, and skin blemishes. The root of the plant has a use too in the treatment of rheumatism and sunstroke - truly a remarkable plant.

Also in the bottom of the hedgerow were still a few clumps of ragwort and thistle in flower, though most of the flowering plants were well over, including willow herb, hedge parsley and travellers joy, but on the verge of the track at one point we found a small creeping plant with a yellow flower which we took to be yellow pimpernel.

Total Distance Walked : 3.5 miles.

Did you know ?

On the hillside immediately to the west is the site of the Comble Roman Villa, the largest Roman house yet found in the Island.

What to look out for

1 Note the long straight bridleway from Havenstreet to Combley. Was this used by the Romans?

2 Between Combley and Duxmore the land is most peaceful, but could it once have been the site of the battle between Jutes and Saxons in A.D.686? Many people think so.

3 Note the old chalk pit dug into the Downs to the south.

4 Note also the Ashey Seamark on Ashey Down to the west.

5 See how many species of hedge plants you can count in the hedgerow north of Combley Farm.

6 Look out in autumn for spindle berries and the brilliant scarlet mass of Black Bryony berries.

Walking Points

1 You can reach the starting point of this walk by car or bus - or even by train!

2 The bridleway from Havenstreet to Combley begins almost opposite the Station car park.

3 The surface of the bridleway is good for walking. Suitable for wheel chairs.

4 To make a circular trip of it fork left after 1/4 mile, and turn right at the first crossroads to Combley Farm.

5 After 1/4 mile on this footpath go through the gate on the right and down the field to the farmyard.

6 Through the farmyard and turn right on to bridleway 18 again back to Havenstreet.

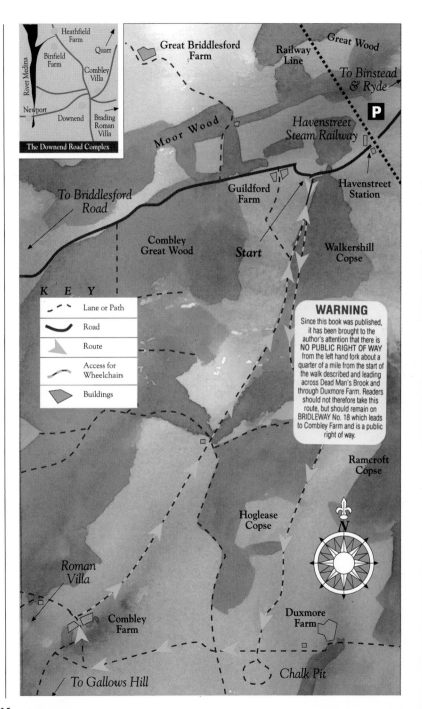

The Downend Road Complex

WARNING
Since this book was published, it has been brought to the author's attention that there is NO PUBLIC RIGHT OF WAY from the left hand fork about a quarter of a mile from the start of the walk described and leading across Dead Man's Brook and through Duxmore Farm. Readers should not therefore take this route, but should remain on BRIDLEWAY No. 18 which leads to Combley Farm and is a public right of way.

When Every Prospect Pleases

 nother short circular walk of about two miles in the Downend / Combley area approached the farm and the site of the Roman Villa from the south, beginning at the point where the track down to the farm leaves the Downs Road. (Map Ref : 536874). This is a sunken track between banks that could perhaps originally have been dug out as a boundary. Each bank has its hedge on top, and a rough count of species put the age at about 900 years. The leaves were beginning to turn and amongst the hedge plants we spotted a spindle tree, its berries glistening in the sunlight. The track led in an easterly direction down the side of the hill past a large disused chalk pit on the right, the slopes of these Downs being pockmarked with these signs of ancient agriculture.

As the slope of the hill began to level out, the track emerged from the shelter of trees and proceeded across a gentle grassy slope towards Combley Farm. We were rather surprised to see notices requesting vehicles and horses to keep to the track and off the grass, but soon we saw that this was obviously necessary as alongside the track was the beginning of another one with distinct traces of both hooves and tyres. At the head of the valley to our left we could see the site of the Combley Roman Villa which is now of course in the centre of the Robin Hill Country Park and not approachable from this direction.

Two hundred yards before reaching the farm the map shows a meeting of four public bridleways, No.90 the one we were on, No.20 to the farm, No.154 to the east and No.155 to the west. This junction is rather puzzling for it is not apparent on the ground. No.20 is the continuation of No.90, No.154 is merely an ill

defined footpath across the fields to Duxmore Farm, and No.155 is apparently no longer extant, the map showing it going up through the woods of Robin Hill. However, this in no way detracts from the peacefulness of the surroundings, and behind a hedge on our left as we walked to the farm the little Deadmans Brook, which rises in springs near the Roman Villa, makes a small lake and then meanders on its way alongside bridleway No.18 to Havenstreet. Incidentally, in this hedge was the most magnificent holly tree, simply loaded with red berries. This whole area has a peculiarly old atmosphere, and is full of exciting possibilities, as mentioned in "A Walk Into The Past". A study of the 1" Ordnance Survey produces some intriguing thoughts about Downend and the various roads and tracks around it. In Roman times when there were no roads such as we know now, Downend, which is just above the Combley Roman Villa, was the meeting point of many important tracks. To the east is the long and fairly straight road along the ridge of the Downs leading directly to Brading Haven, which at that time was a huge protected harbour on the banks of which another Roman built a farm and house at Morton.

To the south another track wound its way down Arreton Shute and thence in a straight line through Merstone and Godshill to Whitwell and the Undercliff. Roman finds have been recorded at Niton and St. Lawrence - curiously enough one particular design of jar has been found here and at Combley - and for centuries myths and legends have surrounded the possibility of a Roman harbour at Puckaster Cover.

To the west from Downend a track (now Burnt House Lane) dropped down to the River Medina at Shide,

Blackberry

and here another Roman Villa has been found, and only a mile or two beyond this lie the sites of yet more Villas at Carisbrooke, Clatterford, and Bowcombe. Slightly to the north of this western track is another one (now Long Lane) which runs down through Staplers to the Medina at its highest navigable point near Coppins Bridge.

To the north east the track that is now the Briddlesford Road - which is itself dead straight in places - heads unerringly to Claybrook Luck at Binfield lower down the Medina, and here for centuries oysters were cultivated, oysters that were first brought to the Island by the Romans. And finally, of all these tracks emanating from the Downend area, we come to Bridleway N.18, the long straight track leading through Havenstreet to the Binstead stone quarries. The theory that all these tracks radiating from this one area are part of a Roman - or even earlier - communications system, connecting a number of Roman settlements with two principal waterways, and with their established fish farms, may be fanciful and lacking in proof, but what an exciting possibility! What is needed is an expert archaeologist to examine the known facts and separate them from conjecture, for what happened in those early days is a fascinating and vital part of our Island heritage.

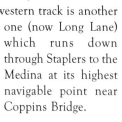

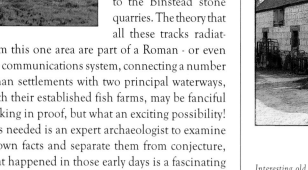

The lane soon began to climb towards Robin Hill. On the way we looked back to this view of Combley.

But let us get back to the walk, through Combley farmyard, which has an interesting old implement shed, we found bridleway no.19 which was the next leg of the walk leading up to the Briddlesford Road at Lynnbottom. This track is not entirely easy to find, for you have to go through a gate and cross a field hoping that at the other side you will find some indication of the route. This in fact proved to be the case and we came to a five-barred gate leading into a little lane through a spinney. Here we paused for our elevenses in this quiet and peaceful corner with only the fields and the trees and the sky as company.

The lane soon began to climb and we found it impossible to go wrong as it led us alongside a tall wire fence marking the boundary of Robin Hill Park. Behind this fence were some ostrich like birds and a few llamas, not at all the sort of fauna you expect to find in the Isle of Wight, but they were equally interested in us and did not mind having their pictures taken. We were hoping to get a picture of the roman Villa site from this position, but alas there was no possibility.

Interesting old farm building at Combley. The barn is built of clunch, with brick quoins and strengtheners.

Entrance to the farm.

As we climbed to the top of the hill by the side of this wire fence it has to be reported that the walk became progressively more disappointing and disturbing, for

we were approaching the Island's principal refuse tip at Lynnbottom, and this is by no means a pretty site. On our right, too, was a high hedge behind which was yet another dump, this one being privately owned and mercifully practically hidden from sight, but all the hedges, and hedge bottoms, and the wire fence, were littered with paper and plastic refuse that had blown off the Lynnbottom tip immediately ahead. On our left behind the fence were no more animals but the Robin Hill scrapyard and dumping ground, littered with piles of old wood, bits of abandoned buildings, all the remains of past tourist attractions, dumped in this once beautiful corner out of sight of their cash customers.

The track we were on debouched on to the Briddles-ford road right opposite the entrance to the Lynnbot-tom Rubbish Tip, and we were faced with a constant

Looking towards Combley Farm from the north-west.

Beech and Harestail Grass

Total Distance Walked : 2 miles.

and noisy stream of lorries and trucks of all shapes and sizes, all bringing in more rubbish. The disposal of modern-day refuse is an enormous problem, and the medieval method of burying it in holes in the ground must sooner or later - and in the Isle of Wight it is likely to be sooner rather that later - come to an end, for there are no more holes left. The floor level of Lynnbottom Copse, once a noted beauty spot, has already been raised several feet, and very soon now a solution has to be found.

Local authorities tell us they cannot afford to re-cycle suitable materials and to incinerate the balance. How soon will it be, we wonder, before they realise that they cannot afford not to adopt such methods.

Feeling rather saddened we hastened to complete the walk back to where we left the car. On the way of course we passed the Hare and Hounds, one of the Island's oldest and most charming thatched pubs. Well, actually, we didn't pass it, for it was almost lunch time and we were in need of restoratives. When we did reach the car we were feeling much better.

Did you know ?

1   There is a whole chain of medieval chalk pits along this edge of the Downs. "Marl" has been put on the land to lighten it from very early times.

2   The word "spinster" comes from the spindle tree, the hard wood of which was used from ancient times for making spindles. At one time it was the unmarried girls that did the spinning, but times change!

3   Another hard wood is Dogwood, and for centuries this has been used for meat skewers. In medieval times dogwood played a much more prominent part in country life than to-day.

4   Dogwood was also knows as the "dog tree", or "dogberry" as its black and bitter berries are not even fit for dogs.

5   "Dogberry" was the name given by Shakespeare to his comic constable in "Much Ado About Nothing".

What to look out for

1. As you leave the Downs Road at Map Ref: 536874 note the sunken track. This often indicates an old boundary of some sort.

2. See if you can spot a Spindle Tree in the left hand hedge.

3. To the right is another old chalk pit.

4. In Combley farmyard note the old implement shed, and the barn built of clunch with brick quoins.

5. When bridleway 19 begins to climb up the hill you may see llamas and ostriches behind the wire fence on your left.

6. You pass fairly close to the Combley Roman villa site in Robin Hill Adventure Park.

7. The Hare and Hounds is one of the Island's oldest pubs, and there are not many now that are thatched.

8. Between the Hare and Hounds and bridleway 90 (where the walk started) notice on the right of the road Moreys Hump, the site of an ancient gibbet. This hill is called Gallows Hill.

Walking Points

1. The Hare and Hounds is a convenient spot from which to start and finish this walk.

2. Leave the Downs Road by bridleway 90 which will take you straight to Combley Farm.

3. Go through the farmyard, straight on up the land (bridleway 19) which soon bends to the left. The bridleway you leave on your right is No. 18 to Havenstreet. Go through the gate on the left and cross the field to another five barred gate leading into a little lane. It is then easy to follow the path to the Briddlesford Road.

4. Bridleway 90 from the Downs Road to Combley is suitable for wheel chairs - but coming back is uphill. Also there is a cattle grid at the entrance to Combley Farm.

5. To make a longer walk of it combine it with Walk No. 5. Turn right out of Combley farmyard on to bridleway 18 towards Havenstreet. Go to where the bridleway forks on the right. (Map Reference 553893) and return by the other leg. This will add 2 miles to the walk.

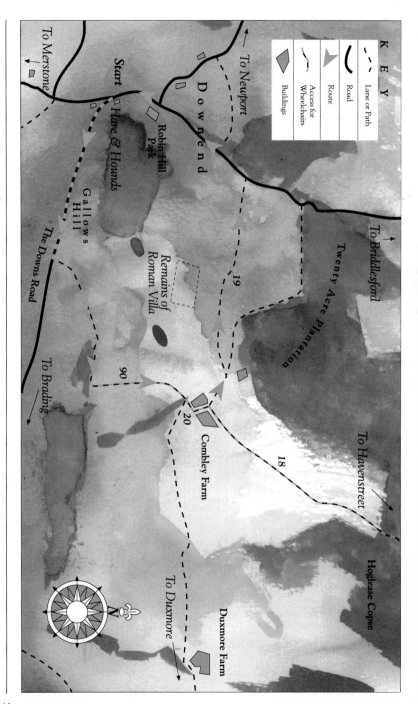

Heads up on Head Down

alking in the Isle of Wight is extraordinary for the variety of scenery that is on offer. There are walks for every taste, every age group, and for every mood. Flat walks, hilly walks, wooded walks; walks for the young and hearty, walks for those who are not quite as young and hearty as they once were, gentle walks for those who have wisely decided to take things just a little easier. The one that is about to be described is a short walk for those who do not want to go too far, or get too dirty, but who need a little exercise, enjoy glorious scenery, and above all want to get out into the open air and blow the cobwebs away.

It starts at Kingates in the south of the Island, not far from Whitwell and close to the delightful little hamlet of Bierley. It involves a little climb and is best tackled on a blusterous day in autumn or spring when there are plenty of clouds scudding across the sky, and nature is very close. The car may be left in a convenient lay-by on the roadside at a point that the map obligingly specifies as being exactly 109 metres above mean sea level. The Map Reference is 511777.

Just across the road from the lay-by is Bridleway No.66 which in its early stages is a well metalled road and is known as Crocker's Lane. Who was Mr.Crocker, I wonder? Kokeritz, who is the authority on Island place names, is silent about this one, but presumably he once lived up here. Perhaps he was related to the John Crocker who gave his name to Crocker Street in Newport in 1341. The first half mile is a stiffish climb rising from 109 metres to 170, so take it easy on this stretch, enjoying the views by stopping frequently and looking back to Whitwell down below in the valley, views that become more stunning the higher you

climb. After a quarter of a mile bridleway 66 becomes No.63, and footpath No.65 forks off to the left - we shall see more of this footpath on our way back. Also on the left are several houses, Hillside Farm, White Lodge, Montana, and a little further on and down another footpath, No.64, a cottage which is well named, The Limit. Here the metalled road ceases and the bridleway becomes a normal track, changing its number to 61, and levelling off. Most of the way so far the track has been in a cutting, with banks on either side - was it once a boundary? Mr. Crocker's boundary, perhaps?

But now suddenly we are out in the open on the top of Head Down, with the wind tearing at our clothes and hair, and stupendous views opening out to the north. The panorama of downs, fields, woods, and farms stretches out mile after mile, and perhaps it is not just the wind that takes the breath away. Slightly west of north and about half a mile away is Downcourt Farm, for many years derelict but now rebuilt, with a bright red tiled roof. Behind Downcourt could be seen the top of the Hoy Monument. Near Downcourt, which is very old and mentioned in the Domesday Survey, three old tracks meet, and here there is a wayside spring with a stone canopy, provided for the refreshment of travellers. Another, almost identical, spring is at Wydcombe less than a mile away. This whole area is a very old part of the Island, carrying a network of ancient paths and bridleways, and while being most remote must have seen many lonely travellers.

Away to the north east the tower of Godshill Church stands out, and as the cloud shadows chase each other across the fields it is brightly lit by the sun. Further off

Red
Dead-nettle

still, and about 6 miles away, the white chalk scar at the top of Arreton Down also gleams in the sun. Whitwell, of course, down in the valley we have left behind cannot now be seen, but behind it is Stenbury, Appledurcombe Down and Gatcliff. Ahead of us to the west the ground rises even further to a height of 237 metres on St. Catherine's Hill. If we continue on this bridleway 61 it will of course lead up to St.Catherine's Down, and the choice of many other and longer walks, but after walking along it some way we decide the time has come to turn back.

A glorious patch of wild flowers in Bury Lane.

The temptation to continue on to St. Catherines was very great, for this is a strange and intriguing area and it is impossible to stand up there on the top of the Down without experiencing a sense of the immensity of nature and our own insignificance. St. Catherines looks down on one of the most dangerous stretches of the Isle of Wight coastline, Atherfield Bay, a stretch that in the days of sail was a notorious hazard for seamen approaching the Island. Atherfield Ledge in its time has destroyed hundreds of ships with the loss of thousands of lives.

In 1313 a French ship carrying a cargo of wine in casks was lost, and much of the cargo was acquired by local people, the Lord of the Manor, Walter de Godyton, being a principal recipient. Unfortunately, the wine had been destined for some religious house, and the full weight of the Church descended on poor Godyton's shoulders. He was not only fined but was threatened with excommunication unless he built a lighthouse on the top of the Down, together with an Oratory in which he was to maintain a priest to trim the light and recite Masses for the souls of those lost at sea.

This he did, the lighthouse was built, and also a cell for the solitary priest to live in. The latter must have had an extremely lonely time up there, but the practice continued right up until the 16th century before being discontinued. Actually, the lighthouse as a warning to shipping was far from successful. The light itself was of course only a wood burning fire, which had a

Gorse in Crocker Lane on the way up to the Down.

restricted visible range, but more to the point was the fact that the top of the Down at 237 metres above sea level was more often than not obscured in mist or cloud, so that the light would be seen by no one but the priest himself. However, a small compensation was that the poor fellow would at least have been able to keep warm.

Having decided to turn back' there were several alternatives for the return route, for here (Map Reference 500775) a number of tracks meet. FP59 goes northwards down the steep side of the hill and is the one to take if you want to go to Downcourt. No.60 drops down more gently to the north east and joins a network of footpaths leading to Couthey Butt, Wydcombe and Bierley. BW61 is, of course, the one we have been following and would take us back the way we came, but the most interesting is FP53 which plunges down the hill southwards straight as an arrow to Niton.

Down Court, with the Hoy Monument beyond.

This footpath, which again is sunken between banks and so could at one time have been a boundary, is called Bury Lane, and the name may be significant coming as it does from the Old English and meaning 'a fortified place'. The point where it meets the other tracks just listed is certainly high and commanding and one wonders if this was once a defended strongpoint high above the very old village of Niton.

In the spring or autumn this path is easy to negotiate, but in summer the vegetation is so lush that in places it is difficult, and when the grasses are seeding it is no place for hay fever sufferers for the grass grows high and has to be pushed to one side. To-day the only problem was with the weather for the black clouds piled up and there were a few spots of rain. For a moment we thought we were in for a downpour, but

the wind was strong and it soon passed over. Half a mile down Bury Lane FP54 shoots off to the left past Ladyacre Farm and immediately starts to climb again until levelling off along the 150 metre contour. In less than another half mile we are back in Crocker Lane again and ready for the last stage of the descent to our starting point at Kingates. Going down the lane and looking across the valley to Appledurcombe Down we decided that with this type of scenery we could easily have been somewhere in the Yorkshire Dales and not in the little old Isle of Wight at all. Gratefully we got back into the car, and only just in time too, for clouds had been massing above us again and suddenly the heavens opened. As we sat there with rain beating down on the roof we talked about this very pleasant little walk, and listed the flowers we had seen on the way. Even in late autumn the Island produces many

Black Bryony berries in profusion.

plenty of berries about, rose, hawthorn, and Black Bryony, the latter having been exceptionally brilliant this year. On the top of the Down we had been rather surprised to find a short stretch of privet hedge, very tall and indeed more like a row of trees than a hedge, but looking in very good condition with not a trace of wind damage or salt burn, in spite of the prevailing sou'westerly wind which often blows up here.

Some of the names of places we have seen are old and interesting. 'Couthey Butt' is made up of 'Couthey' which is a disease sheep get through feeding on wet ground, and 'Butt' which is the piece of land. 'Kingates' is a manorial name first mentioned in 1635 and is possibly the same as 'Kingett' which occurs in Brighstone about the same time. 'Bierley' means 'a farm meadow', though Kokeritz gives some alternative meanings such as 'a swine pasture', 'a barley field', or 'a field with a cowshed'. 'Wydcombe' means 'the wide valley', and Niton, which is mentioned in Domesday under the spelling 'Neeton' is 'the New Farm'. Though no longer new, Niton Manor Farm and the village which grew round it, is still there and flourishing, over 900 years later.

wild flowers, and even with our inexpert eyes we had noted Pink Campion, Herb Robert, Gorse, Ferns, Hedge Parsley, Nipplewort, Dandelion, Black Knapweed, Buttercup and Red Dead Nettle. There were

Fennel, Borage and Tansy

Total Distance Walked : 2 miles

Did you know ?

1 The Hoy Monument was erected by Michael Hoy, a Russian Merchant, to commemorate his happy years of residence in Imperial Russia. It also contains a second dedication, 30 years later, to all the Allied soldiers who fell in the Crimean War fighting against the Russians.

2 The original St. Catherine's lighthouse was 779 feet above sea level, and was frequently shrouded in the clouds. The present light is only 136 feet up, but though it can be seen in most weathers for a distance of 17 miles, the experts have now declared it redundant.

What to look out for

1 As you climb Crockers Lane note from time to time the views behind you.

2 The views from the top of the Down are even better. You can see Godshill church and Arreton Down.

3 Across the valley to the north note Down Court, an old Domesday manor recently restored. Behind it the Hoy Monument.

4 At Map Reference 500775 a number of interesting tracks meet. The one to the south is Bury Lane, which leads straight down the hill to Niton. This point was once probably a fortified look-out position for the defence of the village.

5 Bury Lane is another sunken track, which besides leading up from the village may also have been a boundary.

6 Note the wealth of wild flowers in Bury Lane.

7 If instead of turning down Bury Lane you go straight on, another mile or so will bring you to St. Catherine's Oratory and Medieval Lighthouse on St. Catherine's Down.

Walking Points

1 There is a lay-by for car parking at Map Reference 511777, and a bus stop nearby.

2 Crocker Lane is fairly steep but for the first 1/4 mile or so has a good hard surface. But we hesitate to recommend it for wheel chairs because of the slope.

3 Turn left down Bury Lane at Map Reference 500775 and after about 1/2 mile turn left again at Map Reference 504769 on to FP 54. This brings you back to Crocker Lane and it is then downhill to Kingates.

4 This is a hilly walk, but the superb views from the top are worth the climb.

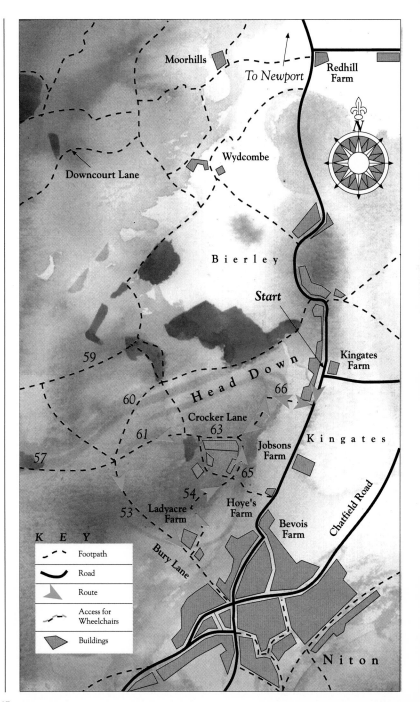

A Pleasant Stroll

We have already explored the bridleways round the Roman Villa at Combley, and from Combley up to Havenstreet, suggesting that this latter track may have been laid down by the Romans for the purpose of bringing stone from Quarr to Combley.

The Romans are known to have developed the stone pits at Quarr from the early days of their occupation, and indeed to have given the district its name, and even to have exported the stone to the mainland via Binstead Hard. The greenish-grey Quarr stone was well known, and was a favourite building material from this time until the quarries became exhausted in the 16th century.

Now we want to explore some of the tracks between Havenstreet and Quarr, for these are equally old and intriguing, and have an added interest in that later on, nearly a thousand years after the Romans were working the quarries, there was another flurry of activity here resulting in the creation of one of the Island's greatest complexes of buildings - Quarr Abbey.

Quarr Abbey was founded in the year 1132 by Baldwin de Redvers, the Norman Lord of the Isle of Wight, the man who also built Carisbrooke Castle in stone. He built Quarr to the glory of God and as an insurance policy against the time when he knew he would have to die. He desperately wanted to go to Heaven, and believed that if he founded an Abbey and installed a number of monks whose only occupation was to pray for his soul, then the Lord would look kindly on him when he arrived at the pearly gates. Whether he succeeded or not we shall never know until we too attempt to join him.

So we have a number of bridleways and footpaths in this area which may have been used by the Romans, and a thousand years later by the monks of Quarr. Now, nearly 900 years later still, we are privileged to be able to explore these tracks and wonder about those far off days and the men who lived and worked here.

The particular footpath we want to investigate is really an extension of Havenstreet itself and starts at the top of the village where three roads meet. In a field just to the north east of this road junction is a large war memorial, and the path goes past this heading as straight as a die for Newnham Farm about half a mile away.

Newnham is old and interesting for it dates back to those 12th century days when Quarr was founded. The present farmhouse is, of course, not as old as that but the site certainly is, Newnham Farm being the home grange, or home farm, of the Abbey which is less than a mile away. The site may well be even older. From the farm we had to walk a few hundred yards along Newnham Lane to a point where it does a very sharp turn to the right to Bartons Corner (Map Reference 570915). This point could well have once been a cross roads with the four arms leading to Newnham Farm, Quarr Abbey, the stone quarries, and Bartons Corner.

And now for a blatant digression from the walk, for which I make no apology. On this latter arm it is possible with a little imagination (very little in fact) to trace a straight route south-eastwards from Bartons Corner via Brickfields, Stroud Farm, Kemphill Farm, Great Upton, Greenlane Farm, Green Lane, Nunwell Farm and across Nunwell Down bang into the Roman

Shepherds Purse

Villa at Morton (Map Reference 600863). One wonders if this was the way they got stone from the quarry to build this particular Villa?

This splendid memorial, in a field above the village of Havenstreet, contains tablets to the memory of the Fleming family.

But the arm we took was the footpath across the fields to the old Abbey. This runs a little west of north gently downhill to the remains of a stream, with no water in it at present, and across a little bridge into Puckers Copse

In the monks' days there was, between Newnham Grange and the Abbey, a chain of small lakes, or fish stews as they were called. Only one of these ponds has survived, but quite close to the little bridge we crossed is a huge man-made bank of earth which must at one time have been the dam of a lake. Below this dam is the one remaining sheet of water, beautifully fringed with trees, calm and peaceful, and when we saw it it was providing a temporary resting place for seven wild geese. Later in our walk we saw them pass overhead on their way to fresh hunting grounds.

On the far side of the next field below the lake, which was contained by its own man-made dam, was the modern Newport to Ryde road crossing the valley on an embankment, and heavily laden with traffic. Could this embankment once have been the dam for yet another fish stew? Beyond it, and a quarter of a mile further on we could see the ruins of Quarr with the Solent behind. What a peaceful spot this must have been before the days of the internal combustion engine and modern roads.

Quarr Abbey was never one of the greater Monasteries of England, but was by far the biggest and most important religious foundation in the Isle of Wight. It was built by monks from the Abbey of Savigny, known as the grey monks, their Abbey being in the Cherbourg peninsular not far from several other Abbeys which were also interested in expanding their missionary work into Britain. Only 15 years later the Abbey of Savigny amalgamated with the larger and more powerful Abbey of Citaux, who were known as the white monks, and of course gave us the name "Cistercian".

Quarr played a very important part in the life of the Island. The Cistercians placed great emphasis on agriculture as a way of life and as a means of funding their religious work, and they practised what they preached. These were extremely hard working and

Pastoral meadows at Newnham Farm.

ingenious in the use of their surrounds. The very small stream which was their only water supply, was dammed at Newnham Farm, creating a sizeable pond. The outlet from this pond was diverted so as to supply the Abbey, leaving the original watercourse to supply the fish ponds they created, the remains of which we had just seen.

The monks expanded their farming activities, and in all set up nine "granges" in other parts of the Island, the very word "grange" of course meaning a granary. So that they contributed in a most practical way to the economy of the district, setting an example of peaceful industry in startling contrast to the ever present threat at that time of baronial warfare.

But the monks of Quarr made another, and possibly even more significant, contribution to life in the Isle of Wight, they helped to look after the poor. In every age there are those who for various reasons find difficulty in coping with life's problems, and are quite incapable of looking after themselves. To such people the monasteries represented a rock on which they could depend when life became impossibly burdensome. No beggar ever rang a bell at a monastery door as was turned away empty handed.

Yellow Iris

Newnham Farm, originally Newnham Grange, the home farm of the Abbey of Quarr.

Quarr Abbey and other monasteries were ultimately closed down on the score that they had become too lax in discipline and too rich, but the community lost out when this occurred and an additional responsibility was thrown on the local parish, for there was no Welfare State.

As we crossed the field, with our minds full of these thoughts, we marvelled at three large and very old oak trees that must have been there for centuries and have seen so many startling changes. Across the road we came into a delightful tree lined bridlepath leading to the Abbey ruins and full of wild flowers and a row of young rowan trees. There were clumps of ragwort, thistle, hemp agrimony, hedge parsley, and several lords and ladies with bright berries. The stream had also crossed the road, by means of a culvert underneath it, and was showing more signs of water as it approached the sea. Along this bridleway we came to

Crossroads at Coppid Hall Farm.

a stone wall running east and west which must at one time have marked the southern boundary of the Abbey grounds. Being human and inquisitive we could not resist following this wall eastwards to see what happened to it.

Sadly, much of the wall has disappeared but there were short stretches where it was still about ten feet high and had its original stone capping. To the eastward it ran into Quarr Wood where it met another wall running north and south marking the eastern end of the grounds. Where the wall crossed the stream there was more vegetation, much woundwort, bird-weed, meadow vetchling and masses of water iris. There were many other wild flowers, and butterflies, particularly the speckled wood brown, and beyond the wall was the blue sky, the Abbey ruins, and the sea.

The monks of Quarr cared for this idyllic spot for 400 years, until it was taken away from them in 1536 by a rapacious King Henry VIII. Could it be that some of the peace and calm that they generated has clung to the spot and is still there? It was with great reluctance that we dragged ourselves away and retraced our steps back up the valley to Newnham.

Total Distance Walked : 3.5 miles.

Did you know ?

1   Every monastery kept fish stews to supply their meatless days. Only one has survived at Quarr, but how many more were there?

2   A special type of Thistle was cultivated in monastery gardens for medicinal purposes. This was called a Blessed Thistle, and was used to treat digestive disorders. It is still an ingredient of some herbal teas.

3   Woundwort was known to the ancient Greeks, and has long been cherished for its antiseptic properties. It is a delicate and beautiful plant which we are lucky to have growing in our own garden, along with other similar delights such as Enchanter's Nightshade and Self Heal.

What to look out for

1   This is a continuation of the Havenstreet to Combley route by which the Romans would have brought stone from Quarr to build their villa.

2   Note the Fleming War Memorial in the field immediately above Havenstreet village.

3   In the meadows beyond the War Memorial we found a large clump of Shepherd's Purse and many other wild flowers and butterflies, suggesting that these fields had not recently been sprayed with week killer.

4   Note the lovely old farmhouse at Newnham, once the home farm of Quarr Abbey.

5   When crossing the fields to Quarr turn off the path temporarily to see the old monks' fish stew on the right.

6   The little lane leading to the Abbey ruins from the main road is delightful, as is the old wall that ran round the Abbey grounds.

Walking Points

1   Leave the car on the verge near the junction of three roads at the top of Havenstreet village.

2   Alternatively, you could start and finish the walk from the White Hart Inn lower down the village. This we confidently recommend, for the food at the White Hart is as good as any in the Island.

3   The path up to the War Memorial is signposted and is fairly steep. Beyond the Memorial is a stile into the next field.

4   Past Newnham Farm turn right into Newnham Lane, and after 200 metres go over a stile on the left into a field.

5   Follow the track north west into Puckers Copse, and in the wood turn right on to the footpath leading to the main Newport to Ryde road.

6   Take care when crossing this busy main road. Go through the gate into a tree lined lane. Suitable for wheel chairs, which can also continue on to the bridleway through the Abbey ruins to Binstead.

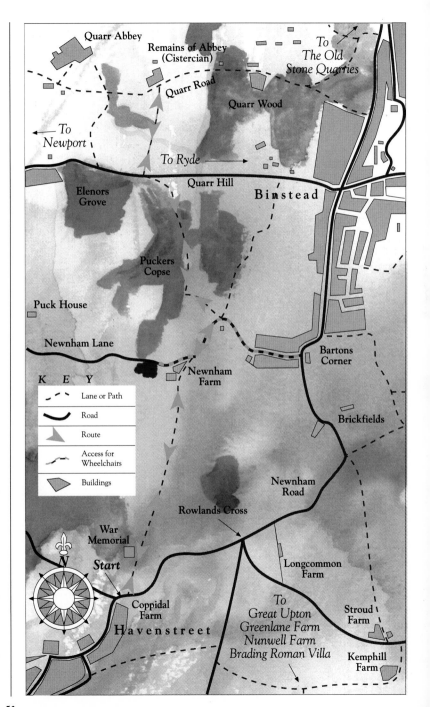

High on a Windy Hill

One of the delightful features of walking in the Isle of Wight is the fact that every outing is different. There are of course many similarities too, for example, the fact that wherever you go the scenery is satisfying and the views superb, and whenever you get on to the high ground there is usually a breeze. If this breeze is blowing from the prevailing sou-westerly or southerly direction then it is coming off the sea and is as fresh and unpolluted as any you are likely to find in the south of England. Good stuff for the lungs, and for giving you the feeling that it is good to be alive in this enchanted land.

But the differences? Apart from the obvious fact that the lowland scenery is different to the upland, that in the valleys there are charming little villages and the odd thatched cottage, while the uplands are high, wide, and windy, with magnificent vistas and sight of the sea, there are other intriguing differences that keep you permanently on the alert. One of the principal of these is the degree of ease with which you can find your way about. Generally speaking the Island is well supplied with public footpaths and bridleways and these are well signposted, so that even the beginner and the novice cannot get lost for long. But it can happen that a footpath can suddenly disappear and leave you flummoxed in the middle of nowhere. Recourse to the map sometimes solves the problem, but sometimes makes it worse, for there is nothing more frustrating than a footpath clearly marked on the map that is simply not there on the ground.

Doubtless there are occasions when an exasperated farmer will plough up a footpath, or divert it, and you have to sympathise with him in his problem. It must be irritating in the extreme to have a public right of way going slap across the middle of your best field that you want to plant with wheat, and at such a time walkers are probably not the farmer's best friends. Were we perhaps in this category one bright October day when we decided on a short 2.5 mile circular walk from Horringford (Map Reference 544854) westwards towards Crouchers Cross and back via Perreton Farm (534855) and Stickworth Hall.

We left the car at Horringford Bridge where the main Arreton to Apse Heath road crosses the eastern River Yar and also the old dismantled railway track. Just north of the bridge is a signpost indicating a bridleway (BW2), and off we bravely set. After about 300 metres we came to a fork. To the left was the drive to Stickworth Hall, to the right the bridleway led to Fulford Farm, which from the map was the right route. A few metres further on a stile on the right hand side led to a footpath heading due north to Arreton village, and on the left a sign saying 'footpath to Merstone' across another field. The bridleway we wanted went straight on , but after 100 metres or so it curved round to the right and led into Fulford farmyard, where the farmer told us there was no right of way. He said to go back to the signpost and cross the field diagonally.

This we dutifully did, avoiding the obvious footpath to Merstone, which was the route we hoped to come back on, and struck off across the field in a diagonal direction. But alas this brought us up against a wire fence and hedge with no apparent way through. There were some enormous mushrooms in this field, and resisting a definite temptation to pick them - the very thought of mushrooms and fried onions making me drool - we cast about for the bridleway we wanted, but

Yarrow

The eastern River Yar at Horringford Bridge. In medieval times there was a mill here.

went off at right angles only 200 metres past Stickworth Cottage, and this would ultimately have brought us back on to the Crouchers Cross route. But we never found this one either, and so pressed on for about half a mile, the way being well defined across gradually rising ground with higher ground to our right. This path then came to a sudden end in the middle of a hedge where a telegraph pole bore a blue arrow pointing to the left, downhill. As this was quite the wrong direction for us we once again went the other way, uphill.

And this was most rewarding, dispelling any frustration we may have felt, for at the top of the rise we found the most stupendous views all the way round. Immediately below us to the north was Perreton Farm, beyond which and a little to the right we could see

without success. Nearby, and on the footpath to Merstone, was Stickworth Cottage, where there was human activity, and they directed us along this path, though this was really not the way we wished to go at all.

At this point a little jingle came into my head that I had learned as a child, and which seemed to be curiously appropriate to the situation we were in. It went something like this -

The engine runs along the rails,
The rails along the ground,
The boiler is full of steam, sir,
And the wheels go round and round.
But what makes the wheels go round, sir
Is more than I can say,
And the signal was dead against us,
So we went the other way!

And this is what we did. We took bridleway BW3 towards Merstone because it seemed the only way, and also because on the map another bridleway (BW8)

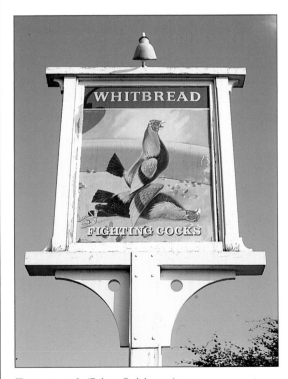

The inn sign at the 'Fighting Cocks', near Arreton.

Arreton village, and behind it Arreton Down. Away to the east was the Ashey seamark, and further round still the white boarded tower of All Saints Church, Newchurch. Westwards was the tall T.V. mast at Chillerton, and immediately to the south a small round hill behind which was presumably Redway Farm.

But what an incredible Island this is, suddenly to produce views like this, vistas topped by limitless skies that send the spirits soaring. How I pity the atheist experiencing this sudden rush of joy, for he has no one to thank. We drank in this scene for some time, finding it difficult to drag ourselves away. Pat took a few pictures, and then we reluctantly began to retrace our steps. On our way back we made a detour to call at Stickworth hall which was in the process of being converted from an hotel into four cottages and twelve apartments A delightfully rural spot in which to live.

So this walk was different in many respects from the others, possibly due to the frustration and bewilder-

*Stinking Mayweed,
Scentless Mayweed
and Creeping Cinquefoil*

ment of finding that the terrain, footpaths and bridle-ways, did not agree with the map. This produced an odd feeling of being in a strange new world of grubbed up hedgerows and obliterated footpaths, and of being intruders in it. And yet we were only a mile or so away

*Stickworth Cottage and
the beginning of
Bridleway No. 3 not
really the way we wanted
to go.*

from Combley and Duxmore which had seemed such a friendly and comfortable neighbourhood, unchanged by time. But then we were separated from them by the high ridge of Arreton Down running from Downend to Brading, and we already knew that the weather could be appreciably different on one side from the other. Perhaps there are other, more subtle, differences.

On this walk we saw very few wild flowers, but amongst them were broad leaved willow herb, common field speedwell, yarrow, scabious, nipplewort, and (possibly) mayweed. In one field there was a herd

The drive to Stickworth Hall.

of black cattle. The high ground we were on is of course helping to protect the Arreton valley from prevailing winds - and this valley has always been the horticultural centre of the Island - where they do say the intensity of light is greater that anywhere else north of Bordeaux!

It was however a delightful walk and one that can be recommended to anyone wanting to get out in the open air for an hour or two without the expenditure of too much energy. The sky was blue, the wind was southerly, not more that force 2, and the countryside was bathed in a mellow October light. Back in the car we only had a mile to go down the road to the 'Fighting Cocks' inn. The nearby crossroads is known as Fighting Cocks Cross, for this area was the centre of cock fighting in the Isle of Wight. Not far away is Wackland, the 18th century home of Farmer Thatcher, and the house where the young bloods of the day gathered to indulge in this rather grisly sport. It is far

Total Distance Walked: 2.5 miles

too fanciful to imagine that some of the atmosphere of those cruel days has lingered on in the area. Or is it?

Did you know ?

1   Nipplewort, which is known to have been growing in England since Stone Age times has flowers that are open only part of the day, closing in the middle of the afternoon, and not opening at all in bad weather.

2   Mayweed, a prolific daisy type flower, does not bloom in May but later in the year. Its name is derived from the Old English name for a maiden as it was once used in the treatment of female complaints.

3   Yarrow has long been venerated for curing wounds. Or indeed for causing them, for in a Gaelic chant a woman says "I will pick the green yarrow that my figure may be fuller, that my voice may be sweeter, that my lips will be like the juice of strawberry. I shall wound every man ...." Wow!

What to look out for

1　At Horringfor Bridge the railway once crossed the road, and the house immediately at the side of the road was the station for Arreton.

2　In the first field we found mushrooms the size of dinner plates.

3　Take time out at the top of the hill to study the views. Look particularly for the following.

4　Perreton Farm down below to the north.

5　The Ashey Seamark to the east, glinting in the sunshine.

6　Also to the east the white weather boarded tower of All Saints Church, Newchurch.

7　Westwards the very tall T.V. mast on Chillerton Down.

Walking Points

1　There is plenty of room to park the car at Horringford Bridge, alternatively there is a bus stop nearby.

2　The start of the walk is bridleway BW2, only a few metres from the bridge.

3　300 metres or so from the start the bridleway forks, the right fork leading to Fulford Farm. On the left is a stile and a signpost that says "Footpath to Merstone". We were told to climb this tile and cross the field, but we never found the other footpath which the map shows leading to Crouchers Cross.

4　We took the footpath to Merstone, passing Stickworth Cottage on the way.

5　Only the portion of BW2 from the main road to Stickworth Hall and Cottage is suitable for wheel chairs.

6　The Fighting Cocks, down the road towards Sandown, supplies good food and has a large car park.

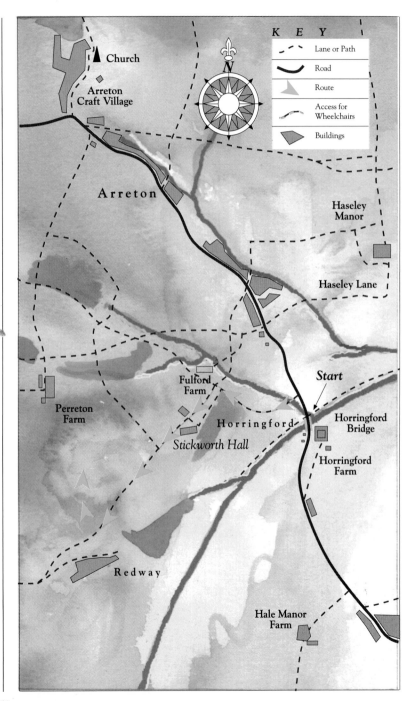

K E Y

- – – – – Lane or Path
- ‿‿ Road
- ▲ Route
- ⌒⌒ Access for Wheelchairs
- ◆ Buildings

Church

Arreton Craft Village

Arreton

Haseley Manor

Haseley Lane

Perreton Farm

Fulford Farm

Start

Horringford

Horringford Bridge

Horringford Farm

Stickworth Hall

Redway

Hale Manor Farm

Crouchers Cross

aving been thwarted in our attempt to walk Bridleway No.2 (BW2) from Horringford to Crouchers Cross by not being able to follow it round Fulford Farm - we determined to tackle it from the other end and start at Crouchers Cross. So one fine morning in December we set out. The sky was blue with slight wisps of cloud here and there; the very best type of December day. And though there was little heat in the sun, what light frost there had been had melted, except in a few pockets of shadow, and these were rapidly disappearing as the sun climbed higher. What breeze there was was from the north, sounds travelled a great distance, and far off there was a slight haze. All things considered, this was a perfect day for walking.

Crouchers Cross is a romantic sounding place name and refers to the crossroads at Map Reference 528859. It is first mentioned in 1470, and according to Kokeritz it probably came about at the time when surnames were beginning to be used, and places were named, either after a particular man, or perhaps from a trade that was carried on nearby. But who Mr. Croucher was is apparently not now remembered.

From the crossroads, to the north lies Arreton Manor and Downend, and the western arm is a continuation of this main road to Blackwater. To the south is East Lane, Merstone, a very minor road nowadays leading to Budbridge, Godshill and the south, and attractive in the complete absence of yellow or white lines painted on its surface. Possibly at one time this straight north to south track led all the way from Downend to Puckaster, and may have been used by the Romans. To the east from Crouchers Cross runs bridleway No.2 (BW2), and this was the route we were after.

As we set out along this grassy track across a huge turnip field there were tremendous views ahead of us and to the south. On our left the ground rose with ever increasing steepness to the high ridge of Arreton Down. The going was easy and extremely pleasant and after just over half a mile we came to a junction where the bridleway was crossed at an angle by a footpath. Just ahead we could see Fulford Farm amongst the trees and it was apparent that the bridleway did in fact skirt the farmhouse. Having satisfied ourselves on this point we decided to go no further in this direction but to try and find the beginning of bridleway No.8 which the map showed as crossing the footpath we had just found.

So off we went along this footpath (FP1) for a little way looking for the turning to the left which should have been bridleway No.8. We never found it, though it is clearly marked on the map as passing through a little spinney, which we explored. After wandering about for a little while we decided that other delights beckoned, and carried on along the footpath which led to Perreton Farm. This path was in fact a wide grassy track, skirting the turnip field in which sheep were feeding, and along the middle of it ran a completely bare track only about six inches wide. We puzzled over this, wondering whether it had been caused by rabbits, or hares, or even foxes, but could see no animal droppings which we would have expected.

At Perreton the pathway turned to the left through a gap in a rather fine stone wall and past two watercress ponds. Through the farmyard a turning to the right took us along the farm drive due west to East Lane. Perreton farmhouse is a comfortable old stone building well tucked in and sheltered, giving the impres-

Herb Robert

.... a rather fine stone wall

latter lane which is the main road from Arreton to Godshill and carries much through traffic.

We turned up the lane in order to get back to FP1 on which we had recently crossed it. There was little traffic about, but I feared for Pat's safety when she insisted on photographing a patch of Herb Robert on the roadside - but after all, it was the beginning of December and unusual to see this very pretty spring flower in bloom.

Once on the footpath we crossed the turnip field, and made our way up East Lane back to Crouchers Cross. Walking up East Lane inevitably reminded me of my theory concerning a possible Roman Road complex emanating from Downend, for East Lane was part of this, and indeed the most controversial part, for it involves the problematical Tin Trade through the Island. It is claimed that long before the Roman

The strange track in the middle of the Bridleway leading to Perreton Farm.

sion of having been there very quietly and peacefully for a very long time. At East Lane, which is the entrance to the farm, the footpath crosses the road and continues due west through another turnip field to Merstone Lane, a very much busier thoroughfare carrying a lot of traffic. Crossing this, FP1 continues for another 300 metres or so across a field which had been planted with winter wheat, showing very green and several inches high, and over a stile into a narrow and old sunken lane. Was this once a boundary?

Crossing this lane we could see Broadfields Farm and Merston Manor slightly to the left, and the footpath headed towards the farm. Here it debouched into Chapel lane, and turning left along this we walked the few hundred metres to Merstone Cross, which is at the junction with Merstone Lane. The village of Merstone is small and is spread out between the Manor House and Merstone Lane. Unfortunately, much of its development has taken place along this occupation of Britain, in fact round about 1100 B.C., the Greeks and Phoenicians regularly visited the British Isles where large deposits of tinstone had been found. Indeed we are told the Greek name for our islands was "Cassiterides" which means the Tin Islands.

This resulted in a regular trade in tin, later taken over from the Phoenicians by the Romans, from the Cornish mines, bringing it along the south coast, crossing to the Isle of Wight, carrying it through the Island to Niton, shipping it to France, and then down through France to Marseilles. This possibility has intrigued historians for centuries, and many opinions have been expressed, ranging from the "absolutely certain" to the "quite impossible". So what is the truth? Was there once a Tin Trade route through the Island, or is it all in the imagination, built up from scraps of circumstantial evidence and strange coincidences into a plausible theory?

Cow Parsley

The grassy bridleway from Crouchers Cross, with turnips to right and to left.

Protagonists of the theory point to the following "evidence". The crossing from the mainland to the Island would have been from Lepe which is close to Stansore Point and Stanswood Bay, "stannum" being the Latin word for tin. The crossing would have been made to Gurnard, which they claim comes from the Latin word "gubernalis", and where until comparatively recently there was a Roman Villa. Various other Island place names 'en route' are claimed to be significant, notably the following - Rew Street, from the French "rue", Gunville from a town in northern France "Gonville" which is also on the route, and Puckaster, from the Latin "castra" meaning a camp. Another local name said to be implicated is buddle (as in the Buddle Inn near Puckaster Cove), a "buddle" being a mining term for a wooden trough used for washing ore. So, who is right? Some say there must have been fire somewhere to have generated so much smoke!

Looking towards Arreton Down from the bridleway near Fulford Farm.

At the top of East Lane, back at Crouchers Cross, we were brought back to more recent events by having the pleasure to meet a stranger who was sitting in his car eating a sandwich. He told us he had lived in Little Budbridge for many years until retirement, when he left to live in Majorca. he had been away five years now but regularly came back, just to enjoy this beautiful part of the Island which he knew so well. Such is the attraction of the Isle of Wight that, though you may leave to live elsewhere, you never forget it.

Refreshed in body and spirit, we had a long look round before leaving, grateful for the opportunities which were continually being given us to enjoy life. We had only walked about 2.5 miles, all of it on more or less level ground, so that we had not had to climb any mountains nor exert ourselves unduly, but we felt better for it.

One final thought. As a sailor I had learned the meaning of Apogee and Perigee, when the Moon is farthest from and nearest to the earth, and feel there must be some significant connection between the names Arreton and Perreton. One of these days I must find out.

Total Distance Walked: 3g miles

Did you know ?

1 *Turnips were unknown in this country before 1550, when they arrived from Holland. They rapidly became a popular food for both humans and animals in spite of their low nutritional value (over 90% water).*

2 *Watercress, which is usually eaten raw or used as a garnish, also makes a delicious soup.*

3 *The Latin name for watercress is Rorippa Nasturtium Aquaticum. An aquatic nasturtium?*

4 *Merston Manor is mentioned in the Domesday Survey, and is one of the Island's many fine old manor houses*

What to look out for

1   East Lane at Crouchers Cross is a lovely country road, no white or yellow lines. Just what a country lane used to be - and should be.

2   The landscape round here is very wide and open, with an enormous expanse of sky and very few hedges.

3   Note the bare track down the middle of the grassy bridleway to Perreton Farm, and the two watercress ponds when you get there.

4   As you reach Perreton, notice the lovely old stone wall.

5   As you pass through the farmyard say hello to the pigs.

6   Note the sunken lane near Broadfields Farm, for this could be an ancient land boundary.

7   Merstone the village is spelt with an 'E', but Merston the Manor without one.

8   If energy permits, walk up the lane for a quick look at Merston Manor. Elizabethan in design, but built largely of brick.

Walking Points

1   Take the grassy track from Crouchers Cross to the east, and after half a mile turn right.

2   Carry on through Perreton farmyard, and the farmhouse drive will take you back to East Lane.

3   Cross the lane and continue westwards, the footpath FP1 being well marked. Cross Merstone Lane and carry on over the next field.

4   Over a stile and cross a sunken lane, then bear left to Chapel Lane. Turn left down the lane to Merstone Cross.

5   Turn left again up Merstone Lane until you reach FP1 again. Turn right and cross the field to East Lane and Crouchers Cross.

6   East Lane is suitable for wheel chairs and there is little or no traffic.

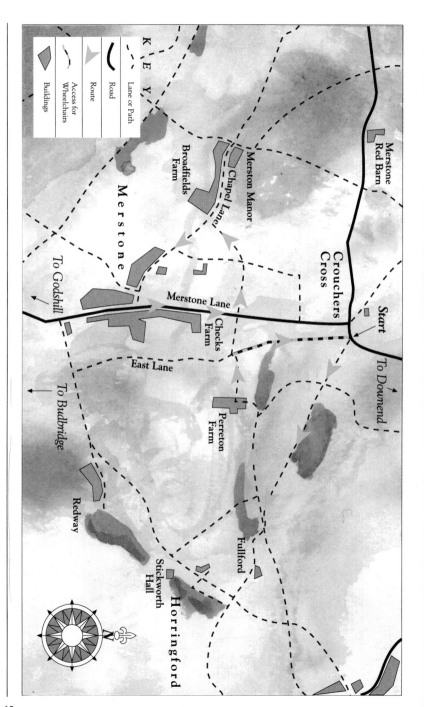

The Past is Always With Us

There is something to be said for walks on the flat, especially if you are getting on a bit and are not as agile as you once used to be. In this situation your principal object must be simply to get out into the open, to breathe the unpolluted country air, and to enjoy the marvellous scenery that the countryside provides for you free, gratis, and for nothing. In the Isle of Wight there are many opportunities of doing just this, along the many miles of old dismantled railway track. God bless Dr.Beeching, some of us might say, though what a wonderful tourist attraction our railways would have been had they still been running! But never mind, their loss is our gain.

We had already walked from Langbridge, near Newchurch, (Map Ref. 559859) westwards along the disused railway track to Haseley and Horringford, but now we decided to go the opposite way, starting from the same spot. Having said this, we then changed our minds slightly, and to make it even more interesting worked out a circular route, saving the flat bed of the railway for the return journey, in case by this time we might be feeling a little weary.

From Langbridge a public footpath (FP9) strikes off slightly north of east along fairly level ground and this was the route we took. This is not a very popular footpath and is far from being well defined, so that care has to be taken not to lose it. Soon after leaving the main road we found ourselves passing through a huge osier bed and though we found it perfectly dry underfoot I could well imagine that in wet weather it might become treacherous. Once having cleared this bed we crossed the fields and after about half a mile came to a little lane that is marked on the map as being an old highway used as a bridleway. The next half mile or so became increasingly interesting for we were entering an area which had a peculiar fascination. Although the route remained flat, all around us the ground was rising and becoming more wooded. But the extraordinary thing was the great feeling of age that we sensed. This was an area where time was standing still, and it seemed impossible that we were still in the 20th Century. Neither of us would have been in the least surprised to have met people dressed in 17th century clothes or to have come across other unmistakeable signs of a bygone age. On our left the ground rose fairly steeply in a series of wooded hills, and we were of course very close to Knighton and the site of its old and mysterious house Knighton Gorges.

Immediately on our left we passed the Old Mill House of Knighton Lower Mill amongst the trees, and soon after this, on the right, was Lower Knighton Farm, both somehow fitting perfectly into the timeless nature of the area. Lower Knighton Mill is believed to have once belonged to Theobald de Gorges, the Lord of Knighton Manor, who in 1365 was appointed Head of the local militia. His family had owned Knighton, and indeed had added their own name of Gorges to it, since 1256, and the Mill as well as Lower Knighton Farm are possibly of equal antiquity.

How much of the atmosphere of this area owes to the sinister reputation of Knighton Gorges it is impossible to say. It could all be in the imagination, for we believe what we want to believe. Shakespeare put it in a nutshell when he wrote -

> "There is nothing either good or bad,
>   but thinking makes it so."

Old Man's
Beard

But Knighton Gorges certainly has a strange reputation, and this seems to have lingered on. It was once the largest and most beautiful house in the Island, but it apparently brought unhappiness to all who owned it, and now its site is said to be haunted. Strange

Alverstone Mill, yet another listed in Domesday.

stories are told that the house occasionally materialises and is seen again with lights shining from the windows, music playing and people dancing. Sightseers still make the journey out to Knighton Gorges on New Year's Eve, which is one of the dates when this is said to happen. The old stone gateposts, which are still there, and have flat round stones on top, are said by many people to have been seen surmounted with heraldic beasts.

These various legends all stem from the 12th century when Knighton was owned by Hugh de Morville, one of the four Knights who murdered Thomas A'Becket in Canterbury Cathedral. He was never brought to justice, and when he died 30 years later was buried in nearby All Saints Church, in Newchurch, in the de Morville family chapel. In the 16th century Knighton came into the possession of Anthony Dillington, and

his descendants lived there for the next 200 years or so, but their history too is not a happy one, and mystery surrounds the death of the last of the line, Sir Tristram Dillington. He is buried in the same chapel in All Saints Church, and his black marble grave slab is there for all to see, but legend says the grave is empty and that he killed himself and is buried in the grounds of Knighton Gorges, since the Church refused to bury suicides.

Whatever the truth of these stories they have persisted through the ages, and you do not have to be psychic to experience the extremely odd feeling of history and fate in what is after all one of the most beautiful corners of the Island. The past is indeed always with us.

On the way back to Langbridge the railway track runs alongside a weed choked river.

After passing Lower Knighton Farm the ancient highway we were on is joined by another bridleway from Knighton, and then meanders on, gradually swinging round to the north to pass through Kern Farm on its way up to Ashey Down. But before this swing took place we left it by a footpath that plunged downhill southwards toward the river valley and Alverstone. Had we continued on the bridleway to Kern it would have added another interesting mile to the walk, but rather hilly, and on this occasion we decided against it.

But Kern Farm is well worth visiting. Perched on the southern slope of the Downs it looks out over the Yar valley and is remote and peaceful. It is one of the manors mentioned in the Domesday Survey, and the

An interesting relic of the past, an old threshing machine at Hill Farm.

Red Campion and Soapwort flowerheads

lovely old stone and tiled farmhouse buildings are pictured and described in "The Manor Houses of the Isle of Wight ". Its name is possibly derived from Quern, meaning a mill, and one automatically jumps to the conclusion that if this is so it must have been a windmill. But behind the farm, covered in brambles, are the remains of a sheepwash, indicating that at one time a stream of reasonable size ran down here. This is now reduced almost to a trickle, but if it was once big enough to be dammed for a sheepwash could it not also have powered a small watermill?

From Kern Farm a pleasant lane runs down past Chiddles Farm to Alverstone, rejoining the route we were taking on our footpath. As we neared the river the woodland became distinctly swampy and I should imagine that some hundreds of years ago the Yar was a very much wider stream than it is to-day. In the woods we were surprised to find both Herb Robert and Pink Campion growing in spite of the fact that we were well into November.

Looking down on Parsonage Farm from the churchyard of Newchurch.

another to Newchurch on the left. By taking this latter path it is possible to add another mile to the walk through beautifully wooded hill country and past Hill Farm.

Further along the old railway the river decides to cross underneath the track and the bridge is a substantial affair built to carry the trains that used to rattle along here. It is not obligatory, of course, to play at 'Pooh Sticks' under this bridge, but if you do I think it only fair to warn you that the current on one side of the stream is much stronger that on the other, so that it is advisable to carry out a little reconnaissance before dropping your stick in the water, or you may get caught - as I was.

From this bridge onwards the track comes out into the open, and it is about three-quarters of a mile back to Langbridge. There are occasional clumps of trees, and the river is never very far away. Altogether a very pleasant and relaxing walk, and at the end of it the prospect of a visit to either the Pointer Inn or New-church Post Office Tea Rooms, both thoroughly to be recommended.

Alverstone, which is also mentioned in Domesday, means 'Alfred's Farm' and is a charming little village, its principal feature to-day being perhaps its old mill. The Southern Water Authority have comparatively recently carried out extensive river control works here, and there is a weir and the pleasant permanent sound of running water. At the foot of the village the old railway line crossed the road, and from here back to Langbridge is an easy 1.5 to 1.75 miles. But this flat and easy path to walk is not without interest. Soon after leaving Alverstone the river, which has been meandering across the fields, comes back temporarily alongside the track, and at one point there is a beautiful spot under an oak tree on the river bank, begging to be used for a picnic. Not far away is a sign warning that the fishing is private, and a signpost indicating a footpath to Alverstone on the right, and

Total Distance Walked : 3 miles

Did you know ?

1 Osiers have been used for centuries in basket and wicker work.

2 Very little is known about the early days of Lower Knighton Mill, but there is reference to two mills in this area in the reign of Richard II (1377-1399).

3 "Pooh Sticks" may be played by young people of all ages.

4 Newchurch Parish was originally very large, stretching from the north coast to the south coast and including the sites of Ryde and Ventnor.

What to look out for

1 Look out for the Osier bed which you cross soon after leaving Langbridge.

2 Knighton Lower Mill House. There are records of a mill here in the 14th century, but it could be even older.

3 This whole area feels very old. Look out for Lower Knighton Farm, another old building on an even older site.

4 If you decide to go via Kern Farm look for the old sheepwash above the farmhouse.

5 Alverstone Mill, which at the time of Domesday was valued at 40 pence.

6 Note the extensive works carried out by the Southern Water Authority.

7 On the way back along the old railway track note the idyllic picnic spot on the bank of the river under a large oak tree.

Walking Points

1 From Langbridge take FP9 eastwards. This footpath is not well defined and can easily be lost. Keep going in a direction slightly north of east and you will reach a junction with a narrow lane listed as an old highway and used as a bridleway, Map Reference 567863.

2 After Lower Knighton Farm the bridleway bears to the right and leads to Kern Farm. FP10 forks right and proceeds southwards. Follow it all the way to Alverstone, the last part being numbered FP53.

3 Turn right in Alverstone, and right again at the Mill on to FP54. Follow this until it joins the old railway track. Take the railway track back to Langbridge, or follow the footpath as it climbs up to Hill Farm and thence back via Newchurch.

4 The old railway track from Alverstone is muddy, but should be O.K. for wheel chairs in dry weather. A bit bumpy though, and there is a stile at the Langbridge end which means that you can't get a chair out.

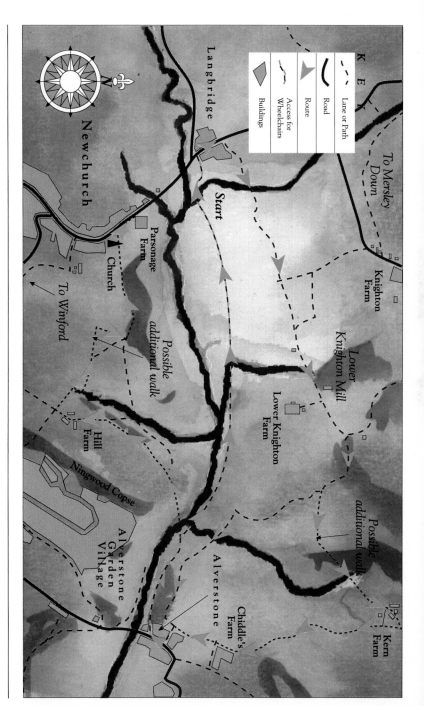

An Historical Tour

istening to the radio and television these days is a pretty depressing business. All the talk seems to be about pollution and the destruction of the environment; in fact nothing but gloom and doom. But here in the Isle of Wight you only have to look out of the window to see a clear and clean unpolluted sky, if you open it you breathe a clean fresh air straight off the sea, and when you go out you are soon surrounded by the myriad greens of the countryside and a profusion of wild flowers everywhere. This year we were treated to a particularly fine display of blackthorn blossom in the early spring, the hedges were white with it, and when this had faded the hawthorns took over and again the eye was dazzled. No sooner was this finished than the wild roses were with us, everywhere great patches of pink and white blossoms in the hedgerows. Oh how lucky we are in this little island!

To get out into this green countryside must inevitably be good for you, and indeed it is the finest therapy known. So here is a typical short circular walk of not more than four miles, which we have walked many times. It may be shortened or lengthened at will, and there are suitable stopping places en route where legs may be rested and thirsts quenched. In addition there are plenty of interesting things to see.

The walk starts near Binfield Corner on the Newport to Ryde road, near the stretch of road known as the Racecourse, (Map Reference 516915). Just on the Newport side of the Corner is an unmade road leading down to the river and signposted to the Island Harbour. This passes through Binfield Farm, which is an intriguing spot if ever there was one. We are told that when the Romans left in the 5th century and the Saxons took over, all the place names were changed, for the Saxons did not think a lot of the Romans. And often, when they found a piece of land that had been cleared and cultivated by the Romans they gave it the name "field". So that it is at least possible that Binfield is of Roman origin and dates back nearly 2000 years. What is more, the track through the farm goes down to the river at Claybrook Luck where the Romans are believed to have farmed their oysters, and where a thousand years later the monks of Quarr Abbey also had a fish farm. On the other side of the Luck is another "field". Heathfield Farm, so that in this area we may be in the presence of great antiquity. Incidentally, the track through Binfield Farm does a double right angle bend, this often being a sign that in Medieval times this was a much larger settlement.

To-day Claybrook Luck contains a Marina, modern and efficient, holding a large number of yachts of all shapes and sizes, the exit to the river being controlled by lock gates operated from a futuristic mushroom shaped tower. To anyone interested in boats it is tempting to stop and wander round, and it is always interesting to watch boats locking in and out. From this point a public footpath follows the river bank, either upstream to Newport, or by crossing the lock gates, proceeding downstream to Whippingham. In wet weather the ground on the other side of the Luck can be very soggy, but this is the only bad patch on the whole of the walk, and once over the stile into the fields the going is good again.

Before leaving the Marina however there are two other items of more recent Isle of Wight history here that are worth noting. The first is the old paddle steamer "Ryde Queen", long since retired from the sea, which

Red Clover

is now berthed here and is a tourist attraction as a public house and night club. The other is that this is the site of a large tide mill, all trace of which has now disappeared. This was the East Medine Mill, one of the largest in the Island, built in 1790 by William Porter, a Newport baker who had a meteoric but brief career as a builder. At the time it was built, convict ships lower down the river were preparing to sail for Botany Bay in Australia, and as Porter's workmen rowed down the river to their work on the Mill, wags on the quayside at Newport taunted them with being bound for Botany Bay. As a result the East Medine Mill became known as Botany Bay Mill, and the nickname stuck. When William Porter built another mill on the opposite side of the river this one was nicknamed Port Jackson Mill.

Reflections in Island Harbour, the old Claybrook Luck where the Romans may have farmed their oysters.

As you walk down alongside the river you can see ahead a small forest of yacht masts from the moorings off the Folly Inn, and beyond them the two tall chimneys of the relatively new gas turbine power station at Kingston. On the right, through the trees, can be seen Medina Park, a large conglomerate of residential Mobile homes, fairly well screened from the view. In a few years time when the vegetation has further thickened, it will hardly be visible at all.

The Folly Inn has one of the finest sites of any pub in the Island with a terrace fronting the river, against which the tide laps gently at high water. The original Folly was a boat moored in the river, and in the 18th century this became a fashionable resort for the young bloods of the Island, the site being sufficiently remote for them to be able to misbehave themselves without annoying anyone else. Gradually the boat fell into disrepair, and when it reached a sinking condition it was hauled ashore and continued its career dryshod. Subsequent repairs and alterations meant that it became more of a building than a boat, and when the ramshackle limit was ultimately reached it was rebuilt. To-days building is well found and efficiently arranged, though alterations, mainly of a cosmetic nature, continue to be made as fashion and the owner's whim dictate. It is a good spot in which to stop and, if weather permits, to sip one's drink on the terrace while watching the yachting activity in the river.

From the Folly it is necessary to walk up the road a little way until one of the three entrances to Medina Park is reached. Here on a sharp bend in the road a footpath plunges into the woods on the left. The next half mile is truly delightful walking, through this small

Common spotted orchid. These not-so-common flowers abound in the fields of Whippingham.

wood and then across the fields to Whippingham Church. There are four stiles to climb on the way, but these are not difficult, and there is plenty of interest. In the first field, on the left of the path, the ground has not been cultivated for some years, and hence there is a wealth of wild flowers. From a very superficial examination, one day at the beginning of June, we saw birdsfoot trefoil, clover, buttercup, ox-eye daisies, a vetch (not yet in full flower), at least two different types of wild orchid, and even a wild rose bush, which is a rather strange thing to find in the middle of a field. On the right of the path buttercups predominated and were a magnificent sight. Having a field day amongst all this blossom were a number of common blue butterflies - only called a "common" blue, but what a glorious colour they are!

As the ground rises towards the church you see more and more of the river away to your left. The river Medina, as its name implies, cuts the Island in two, running from north to south from the Solent up to Newport which itself originated in the 12th century when the Norman Lord of the Island built "a new port for his castle of Carisbrooke". There are many yacht moorings in the Folly Reach, and almost opposite the inn is a small creek at Werrar which is possibly the site chosen by the Vikings (c.A.D.1001) for their winter encampment when they first decided not to return to Scandinavia after their summer raids on the Isle of Wight and adjoining mainland.

Whippingham itself is a very ancient settlement, the first record being in the year 725, its name meaning "the homestead (or river meadow) belonging to Wippa's people". But to-day Whippingham means Queen Victoria, for the church was designed for her by her beloved Prince Albert and she worshipped there regularly for many years. Albert's church is the third on this site, the first being Saxon, and the second having been designed and built by John Nash, the celebrated architect who made his home in East Cowes. Nash's church was not a success and the Prince Consort felt no compunction in pulling it down and erecting something more worthy of his Queen and Empress. It is a strange but imposing building and one that would not look out of place in Albert's own Germany. The church retains its original dedication to St. Mildred, an Anglo-Saxon Prin-

cess and Saint who hailed from the Isle of Thanet, that other off-shore island near the coast of Kent that, together with the Isle of Wight, was first invaded by the Jutes. The Royal Church of St. Mildred is well worth a visit for it is full of treasures and Victorian memorabilia. Princess Beatrice, the Queen's youngest and favourite daughter was married in this church to Prince Henry of Battenberg in 1885. Both she and her husband became Governors of the Isle of Wight in their turn, and they are both buried here, side by side. In the surrounding churchyard there are several other interesting graves, including those of Prince Louis of Battenburg and Princess Victoria of Hesse, parents of the late Earl Mountbatten, and grand-parents of Prince Philip, Duke of Edinburgh.

From Whippingham Church several interesting alternatives for a continuation of the walk present themselves. You could of course retrace your steps across the fields and water meadows, downhill all the way to the Folly and then level going to Binfield Corner, but if this is felt to be too unenterprising you can walk up the road from the church to the first corner. Here a footpath continues across the fields to Barton Manor (three quarters of a mile) and/or Osborne House (1 mile). Both are of course Royal residences closely associated with Queen Victoria, and both compulsive viewing. Indeed, they are both so important and fascinating, that you cannot possibly do them justice as part of the present walk. They both warrant a special visit, and to enjoy them to the full each should be given a full day.

So instead of taking this footpath, continue along the road, Beatrice Avenue, towards its junction with the main Newport to East Cowes Road, (a quarter of a mile). On the way, on the right hand side of the road you will find the entrance to Padmore House, one of the Island's finer restaurants and hotels. Here the weary traveller may relax in the oak-panelled bar, and in the dining room find immaculately laid tables, first class service and excellent food, all preceded by a

Moorings in Folly Reach, Medina River.

Ox -eye Daisy
and Meadow Buttercup

Total Distance
Walked : 4 miles

friendly welcome from mine host. Padmore House is a gastronomic oasis in this part of the Isle of Wight. Having ultimately reached the main road you may take advantage of the frequent bus service which in no time at all will whisk you back to Binfield Corner, or on to either Newport or Ryde. But should you wish to walk a little further, perhaps fortified by the lunch at Padmore House, cross the road at Whippingham Forge and walk along Alverstone Road to Dallimore's Corner (half a mile). From Dallimores it is then a pleasant walk of almost exactly one mile along country roads to Binfield Corner.

In a way, this walk is a mini-historical tour, for in no more than four miles walking you will have had a brief contact with the Romans, the Jutes, the Vikings, the Norman monks of Quarr, an historical riverside inn, and possibly the most famous of all the many Queens of England. And pervading all, colouring it, unifying it and giving it its character, the deep peace and tranquillity of the immemorial fields and woods, a countryside that has seen all this ongoing historical pageant of human activity, and has so much to give us in return.

Did you know ?

1 . The first meadow after leaving the Folly is full of wild orchids in early summer, hundreds of them. As well as many other flowers.

2   Uffa Fox lived for a time in a converted Cowes Floating Bridge moored just above the Folly, and then built a house which is now in Medina Park.

3   Padmore House, which looks down over the river, was once the home of the Vicar of Whippingham and is now a successful country hotel and restaurant.

What to look out for

1. Binfield Farm, a very old settlement.

2. Island Harbour, originally Claybrook Luck. Here is the Ryde Queen and many assorted yachts and yachtsmens houses. Here also is the site of the East Medina Mill, built by William Porter. And earlier still the Roman oyster farm.

3. Look down the River Medina and imagine the boatloads of men being taken to the convict ships bound for Botany Bay.

4. The Folly Inn is a good spot from which to watch the boats go by.

5. In Whippingham water meadows look across the river to a creek where the Vikings first wintered nearly a thousand years ago.

6. Another more recent grave is that of Uffa Fox, yacht designer and sailing companion of Prince Philip.

7. Whippingham Church, designed by the Prince Consort for Queen Victoria. The church may be locked, but the churchyard contains some interesting graves of well known people.

Walking Points

1. From Binfield Corner follow the unmade road to Island Harbour.

2. The public footpath crosses over the lock gates near the mushroom shaped control tower.

3. Follow the footpath down the river bank to the Folly Inn.

4. Go up the lane from the Folly and turn left into the woods at the entrance to Medina Park. Follow the footpath up to Whippingham Church.

5. From the church walk along Beatrice Avenue, a quiet country road, to the right, and you come to the main Newport to East Cowes road. Cross this and turn left along Alverstone road.

6. Take the first turn right at Dallimore's Corner, and go down the hill, crossing the main road again. Carry straight on back to Binfield Corner.

7. The first part of the walk, from Binfield Corner to Island Harbour, is suitable for a fairly robust wheel chair, and there are many interesting boats to be seen there.

8. The country roads have good, if rough, surfaces for wheel chairs, but do beware traffic.

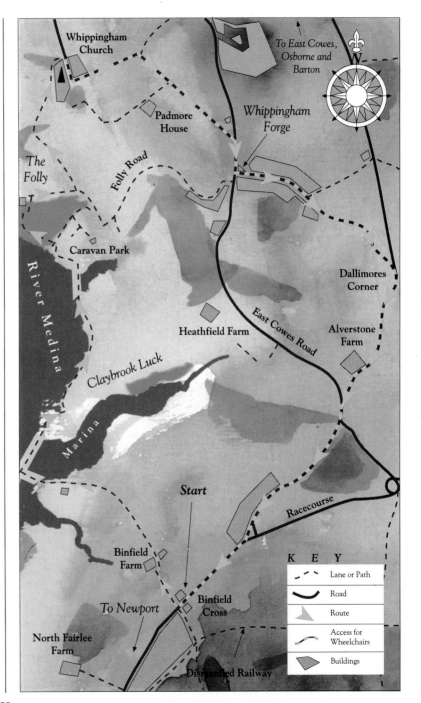

Whippingham Church

To East Cowes, Osborne and Barton

Padmore House

Whippingham Forge

Folly Road

The Folly

Caravan Park

Dallimores Corner

River Medina

Heathfield Farm

East Cowes Road

Alverstone Farm

Claybrook Luck

Start

Marina

Racecourse

Binfield Farm

To Newport

Binfield Cross

North Fairlee Farm

Dismantled Railway

K E Y

- - - Lane or Path

Road

Route

Access for Wheelchairs

Buildings

An Ancient Highway

The National Trust Car Park just off the Calbourne to Brighstone road, and about midway between the two villages, is very strategically placed for walkers and those who want to explore the surrounding area of downland, an area that has been inhabited by man as long as any part of the Isle of Wight. The Car Park's map reference is 420845 and it is situated slap on one of the Island's oldest of its many ancient highways, the one that runs from the Needles in the far west to the River Medina where Newport now is. It crosses the river by the first ford, and connects up with routes to all the eastern parts of the Island.

From this Car Park it is possible to find, within reasonably easy reach, the Longstone at Mottistone, a Jutish burial ground at Shalcombe, the site of the Roman Villa at Rock near Brighstone, and a host of Bronze Age tumuli. And from this starting off point the number of other interesting walks that may be made is legion, walks to suit all tastes and all requirements, long ones, short ones, forest walks, downland walks, and all at some stage or another offering breathtaking views of countryside and sea.

This type of countryside, with its wide vistas and feeling of great age, is perhaps at its best on those crisp days in autumn or spring when the air is like wine and the landscape is bathed in a light that promises a settled and glorious day. And it was on just such a day that we decided on a circular walk of moderate length - just under three miles - starting from this convenient spot provided by the National Trust.

Now it has to be admitted that whenever we begin a walk from this spot we experience a curious feeling of elation and anticipation. It isn't that we expect to find anything particularly startling or world shaking on our way, but there is something in the atmosphere of the area, something perhaps to do with the extraordinary age of this old highway which has been here since the Island began, that communicates itself to us. We experience a feeling of somehow - perhaps only temporarily - slotting into our Island heritage, and we know that the next few hours of our lives are going to be exhilarating, enjoyable, and rewarding.

As we left the Car Park, having put on our walking boots and shouldered the little pack that contained what we considered to be essential equipment (we tend to carry everything with us except the kitchen sink) the sun was already well up, and though there was a nip in the air its warmth was beginning to get through and we could tell that by mid-day it would be as warm as anyone could wish for when walking. There had been a heavy dew overnight, and earlier the fields had been wreathed in mist, but this had already now been burned up by the sun.

The Calbourne to Brighstone road is known as Lynch Lane, the meaning of 'Lynch' being 'rising ground', for it rises to cross the ridge of the Downs that separate the two villages. As we left our starting off point on this ancient east to west highway we crossed over Lynch Lane and were heading in an easterly direction, climbing steadily as the track rose to the top of the Down. Underfoot the going was good, the surface being of hard chalk and very well defined. Immediately on our left was the edge of Brighstone Forest which in this area was mainly deciduous trees, though large sections of the forest have been planted with conifers. But on our right a view was already beginning to

Tufted
Vetch

unfold, a view that made the heart beat a little quicker and demanded attention. The Isle of Wight is famed for its huge panoramas of land and sea and sky but this view we were now seeing from this ancient road is one of the most spectacular. Maybe the upward

The old highway looking towards Mottistone Down. You can see the edge of the wood in the distance that it follows.

climb of the track contributed to the feeling of breathlessness that we both experienced but we frequently had to stop just to gaze at what we could see.

The ground falls away rapidly to the south, and immediately below was the village of Brighstone, old and picturesque with its thatched cottages and homely village church. At one time called Brixton, this village is now firmly on the tourist route and attracts many coachloads of visitors in the season. Beyond Brighstone was the sea, and indeed, as we climbed higher, it was the sea that dominated the view. Looking back westwards, across the rolling downland to Mottistone Common and Compton Down we could see Tennyson Down and the tall white cliffs of Freshwater Bay. To the east the view was equally grand, embracing the wide sweep of Atherfield Bay, and beyond it the high ground of St. Catherine's Down.

After about three quarters of a mile the bridleway forks, one arm going straight on to cross Limerstone Down, but the other passing through a five barred gate on the left into Brighstone Forest (432842). This was the route we had to take, but for a moment we paused to take one long last look at the tremendous stretch of land and sea that was spread out below us. As we stood there in the already warm sunshine with a pleasant breeze blowing in our faces the only sound we could hear was the faint barking of a dog in Coombe Farm, half way down the hill towards Brighstone.

Almost reluctantly we turned and opened the gate. But we were now entering one of the most interesting and intriguing parts of the Isle of Wight, an area of lost ancient villages that are believed to have been thriving almost 3000 years ago. The whole district is criss-crossed by a network of old bridleways and footpaths which once were an important part of Island communications. There is little to be seen now of this erstwhile human occupation, and the planting of the forest by the Forestry Commission has effectively covered up most of the archeological remains.

Part of Brighstone Forest that was wrecked by the hurricane. The Triangulation Point is on the right.

A short walk of only a hundred yards or so brought us out into the open again into a large area that has had to be replanted following the damage caused by the hurricane of 1987 that tore its way across the Island. At this point Bridleway No.9 shoots off to the left and, it you want a shorter walk, it will take you down through the forest to Calbourne Bottom on Lynch Lane and hence back to the Car Park, a total distance of one and three quarter miles. This is a lovely walk through the woods, but we had decided to go a little further before returning, and continued on up the track for another 100 yards or so to a junction where five tracks meet.

Walking up this part of the track in this recently devastated area it is impossible not to be affected by a sense of age and mystery and long departed human activity. What were they like, the people who lived up here in those remote days? Were they happy? Or were they like so many of us, restless and discontented? What problems did they have? Surely these must have been different to ours, but no doubt just as harrowing. Did they ever worry lest the sun should not rise again as usual next morning? Were they frightened by thunderstorms, when it must have seemed to them that the gods were angry? We paused, half expecting to discover the truth, but there was no voice, nor any that answered, only the deep peace of this slumbering spot which enveloped all.

There is a signpost at this five-fold junction indicating that Bridleway No.4 goes straight on and in approximately four miles would bring us off the Downs into Carisbrooke. To the right Bridleway No.1 leads through Fern Bottom and Rowborough Bottom to Rowborough Farm which lies on the Carisbrooke to Shorwell Road in the beautiful Bowcombe valley, two miles distant.

But our route lay along Bridleway No.8 which is signposted to the Calbourne to Brighstone Road one mile away. The ground here is still rising though we were now nearing the top of Brighstone Down, and indeed, a quarter of a mile further on and just to the right of the track is a triangulation point marking the highest spot, 700 feet above sea level. Here, on top of the world, the ground levels off and the track is grassy and very pleasant for walking. Soon after passing the triangulation point the forest starts again, through a tangled fringe of uptorn trees that bear silent witness to the horror of the hurricane. The wood from now on is mainly beech and very attractive, and the bridleway is crossed by several paths and forest rides, one of which is the boundary between Brighstone and Calbourne parishes. Where it crosses is a wide open grassy place, and the continuing bridleway is a little difficult to pick up as it enters the wood on the other side.

Here the number of the bridleway changes from 8 to 20, and it plunges downhill through the wood, as straight as a die for a quarter of a mile and then out through a gate into a large meadow. The views form this gate to the north-west are splendid, out over the village of Calbourne and Newtown harbour to the wide expanse of the Solent, a glorious stretch of countryside. The bridleway rather loses its identity as it leaves the wood, but is marked by a line of very old and gnarled hawthorn trees down through the meadow. We have seen similar rows of old hawthorn in other parts of the Island and they invariably indicate the existence at one time of a bridleway or highway. This meadow, incidentally, in summer is full of wild flowers, red and white clovers, vetches, self heal, lesser stitchwort (great patches of this with its beautiful star like flowers),buttercups, daisies, thistles, ragworts and many others.

At the bottom we passed through a gate into a narrow lane, having in just under half a mile dropped about 500 feet, and we were soon once more on the Calbourne Road. To return to our starting point we now had a walk of about three quarters of a mile along this road, Lynch Lane. This is by no means an unpleasant

The deserted farmyard at Gotten Leaze.

secrets does this little complex of buildings hold? Its name too is slightly mysterious. Gotten Leaze is thought to have been originally Gotten Lease, so called because it belonged to the Manor of Gotten in Chale, or was leased by them. Further on the road re-enters the forest, reaches Calbourne Bottom, and begins to rise as it nears the saddle taking it over the Down to the south. This is a winding and beautiful, but lonely stretch of road through the woods, and we were rather surprised to meet a woman and two small children walking down the hill. She was carrying a basket containing sandwiches and a flask of tea for her husband who was working in the fields, and she gave us a friendly "good-day" as we passed. In the distance we could hear the sound of his tractor.

The last few hundred yards to the top of the hill were steep and we had to take them slowly, and it has to be said that we were glad to get back to the car and sit down. Walking along a road is hard on the feet. Finally, as with all our walks, we like to be able to recommend one of the Island's many charming village inns where well earned refreshment nay be obtained, and on this occasion there is a choice of two, either the Sun Inn at Calbourne or the Three Bishops at Brighstone. Both of these can supply good food for the weary traveller in pleasant surroundings, and are very satisfactory places in which to sit for a few minutes remembering the walk and being grateful for all the beauty that this Island of flowers has to offer.

part of the walk for the lane is rural and out of the summer season carries very little traffic. It is in fact a typical Island country road, undisfigured by painted lines which seem to be so necessary to show the motorist where he is.

On the left, soon after leaving the bridleway, was the mysterious and rather eerie deserted farm of Gotten Leaze. A large stone barn and other outbuildings, derelict and forlorn, and the farm house, windows and doors blocked up, the garden waist high in grass and weeds. It was abandoned many years ago - what

Oxford Ragwort

Total Distance Walked : 3 miles.

Did you know ?

The Island is covered by a network of old paths and tracks. Some of these have been incorporated into modern roads, but many of them are tucked away in the countryside and can only be found on foot.

What to look out for

1 Stop frequently as you climb the track up from the car park, turn round and admire the view westwards over Mottistone Down, and southwards over Brighstone to the sea.

2 At the top look back and see Compton Down, Tennyson Down, and the cliffs at Freshwater. Look eastwards to Atherfield Bay and St. Catherine's Down.

3 Find the Triangulation Point, 700 feet above sea level, and surrounded now by replanted forest..

4 Feel the age of this Brighstone Forest area, and imagine the many people of old who lived up here.

5 Just before you reach the Triangulation Point note the five-fold track junction, an ancient crossroads on top of the world.

6 As you come out of the forest on the northern side there are fine views towards the Solent and the mainland. You can pick out Newtown Harbour.

7 Gotten Leaze, deserted and eerie.

Walking Points

1 From the National Trust car park the bridleway to the east is uphill for 3/4 mile. The surface is good, but one hesitates to say it is suitable for wheel chairs because of the slope. But the views from the top are spectacular and worth a lot of effort.

2 From the gate into the forest the gradient is not so great, but the surface is perhaps a little rougher. The gates are openable.

3 The Triangulation Point is a few yards to the right of the bridleway, which continues on into the wood and is fairly easy to follow all the way down to the Calbourne Road.

4 One tricky spot is where the bridleway crosses a wide grassy place about 250 metres from the triangulation point. Here the entrance into the wood on the opposite side of the open space is a little difficult to see.

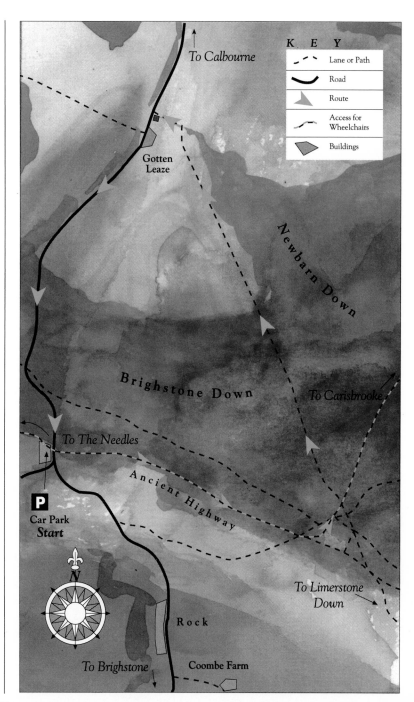

To Calbourne

KEY

Lane or Path
Road
Route
Access for Wheelchairs
Buildings

Gotten Leaze

Newbarn Down

Brighstone Down

To Carisbrooke

To The Needles

Ancient Highway

P
Car Park
Start

N

To Limerstone Down

Rock

To Brighstone

Coombe Farm

Centurion's Copse to the King's Town

The Isle of Wight contains many mysterious areas, places where events of long ago and long departed people have left behind an atmosphere of uncertainty, mystery, and legend. None is more mysterious than that part of the Island between Bembridge and Brading, much of which area was once covered by the sea and was known as Brading Haven. Here the centuries have seen enormous changes in the actual shape of the land, and it is now possible to walk dryshod all the way from Bembridge to Brading across the bed of the old Haven, and this was a walk which, one fine summer's day, we decided to make.

We parked the car by the side of the road, and just off the carriage way so that it was not causing an obstruction, at Map Reference 626867. This point is quite near Bembridge Airport on the Brading Road and marks the beginning of a public footpath known as Centurion's Lane. And this is the start too of the first mystery, for this little footpath goes gently downhill for a quarter of a mile and at the bottom is Centurion's Copse. The wood is beautiful, rather tangled, impenetrable in places, and full of wild flowers, wild garlic and pink campion predominating on the day we were there.

The name "Centurion" suggests that the wood has Roman connections, and though this may be so - for in every part of the Island there are traces of Roman occupation - the derivation of the name is even more mysterious and curious. This area is believed to have been the site of the Manor of Wolverton and a village of the same name, but both were destroyed by the French, possibly in their major raid in August 1377. The Norman Lords of this Manor at one time were members of the Clamorgan family, and one of them had a son Nicholas de Clamorgan who was classed at that time as an "imbecile". This may be the reason why the private Chapel of the Manor was dedicated to St. Urian, the patron saint of the mentally handicapped. And from St. Urian to Centurion is a very small step indeed.

We would like to have found the site of this Chapel, but alas the area is so overgrown now that it would probably need a full scale professional investigation to locate it. We wandered off the path into the wood and were soon sidetracked from our search by the wealth of wild flowers that we found. Also the site is very boggy in places, and after getting our feet wet we ultimately decided to let the mystery remain and to continue our walk.

Another fascinating thing we would dearly love to have found was a reputed Holy Well, for we had read about this in the memoirs of Sir John Oglander written at the beginning of the 17th century. He asserted that at one time in the past Brading Haven had been dry land and that it was through neglect of the sea wall in the 13th and 14th centuries that the sea was able to break through. He claimed that this was substantiated by the fact that when the haven was drained in 1594 a stone lined well was found. This well subsequently was drowned again when the sea wall collapsed in 1630, and did not come to light again until 1878 when railway engineers finally succeeded in building a solid embankment and channelling the waters of the River Yar which previously emptied into the Haven. But no one now seems to know quite where the well is situated though there are several theories, even one that says there must be two

Field Bindweed

wells, for Oglander's well and the Holy Well in Centurion's Copse cannot be one and the same. Having splashed about in some of the soggy parts of the wood, and also having examined the earthworks

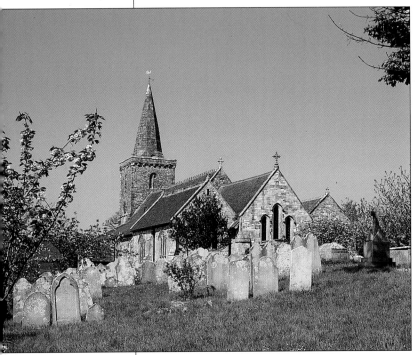

Brading Church from the South East.

on the northern side, which some say are the remains of a harbour wall, and others maintain were thrown up by a large party of French raiders who landed here in 1545, the day after the "Mary Rose" sank, we left the wood and carried on for another quarter of a mile to the Great Sluice (Map Reference 620870). Here we finally emerged from the shelter of trees and bushes and climbed a stile out on to the embankment which was built in 1594 in an attempt to reclaim the top half of the Haven.

The Great Sluice is described on the Ordnance Survey map as being disused, but for many years it must have played a major part in the draining of the marshes and

the controlling of the River Yar, one arm of which passes through it. There is a very fine stone built culvert here of Victorian age, and from the stile you look out over the old Haven to Brading on the other side. The path now runs along the top of the embankment and it is a little over a quarter of a mile to the beginning of Wall Lane in Brading, crossing the other arm of the river by a farm type bridge.

With a little imagination it is possible to see what this part of Brading looked like in the days when the sea came right up here. Wall Lane is in fact the edge of the harbour wall, but immediately to the south, instead of water we now have a modern housing estate. At the town end of the wall, nearly half a mile from where we came on to it, is the centre of old Brading - the church, the town hall, the high street, and one of the oldest houses in the Island (now the Osborn-Smith Wax Museum).

Brading is a very old settlement indeed, and in 1280 was given a Charter by Edward I, since when it has often been referred to as "the King's Town". Edward I, that very astute and warlike king, always kept a wary

A riot of pink campion and other wild flowers in Centurion's Copse

eye on the French and was alive to the danger of them invading England through the Isle of Wight. Consequently he was determined to control the two great Island harbours, Brading Haven and Newtown, both of which were vulnerable. Hence his interest in giving Brading a Charter, and his subsequent commandeering of Newtown Harbour from the Bishops of Winchester in 1285.

The Church, dedicated to St. Mary, is one of the oldest and most beautiful of all the old Island churches, and it is a favourite of ours. We never come to Brading without visiting the church, though on this occasion we deferred our visit until after we had eaten, for we were hot, hungry and thirsty. Fortunately we did not have far to go, for only a few yards down the road was the Bugle Inn, an ancient hostelry that has been brought up to date and serves good food. The Bugle gets its name from the heraldic arms of Henry Beauchamp, son of the Earl of Warwick, who in 1445 was crowned King of the Isle of Wight by his friend Henry VI. His coat of arms included a young bullock - in Latin "bucullus" - from which comes the word "bugle". The musical instrument of this name is said to make the same noise as a young bullock!

We did visit the church before starting off on our homeward journey, and automatically made our way to the Oglander Chapel. The Oglanders lived at nearby Nunwell for over 800 years, and a number of them are buried in the Chapel, Sir John Oglander, the most famous, among them. It is to Sir John, of course, that we owe practically all our knowledge of life in the Isle of Wight during the first half of the 17th century for he noted down everything that interested him, and fortunately these writings have survived. His tomb is in the Chapel , and those of his father and grandfather, and there are many other memorials to members of the family, one in the form of a beautiful copy of Michaelangelo's "Pieta", the original of which is in St.Peter's in Rome. A few years ago Pat took a photograph of the "Pieta" one October afternoon

when the sunlight was streaming in through one of the stained glass windows, and the result which was published in our book "Village Churches of the Isle of Wight", was magical.

Tomb of Sir John Oglander in Brading Church. He bought the effigy in France and when he died left instructions that it was to be mounted on his tomb.

On most of our walks we like to arrange a circular route, but to-day, in order to keep the walk to manageable proportions, we retraced our steps and returned the same way. The distance each way was about 1.5 miles and as we had spent some time exploring in Centurion's Copse, we reckoned that by the time we got back to the car we should have covered about 4 miles, which seemed to us to be a very satisfactory distance. As we walked back along the embankment we discussed the history of this remarkable area which has seen so many changes and has played such an important part in the Island story. The Romans inevitably used the harbour when the 2nd Legion occupied the Island, and later some very influential Roman built the luxurious villa at Morton overlooking the Haven.

One of the oldest houses in the Island, now the Osborn-Smith Wax Museum.

Common Field Speedwell, Brooklime and Lousewort

Total Distance Walked : 3.5-4 miles

In the 9th century King Alfred the Great is believed to have fought a decisive battle with the Danish invaders in Brading Haven and to have driven them off. The fortunes of Brading as a town have always been closely linked to the Haven, and once this began to silt up so the town began to decline. The harbour became marshy and several attempts were made to accelerate the process of draining it and turning it into pasture, but the sea proved reluctant to leave, and it was not until the coming of the railway in 1878 that this was satisfactorily achieved. Once this was done however Brading relapsed into the charming and peaceful old town that it is to-day.

As we walked back across the embankment we reflected that Brading's loss was our gain, for the Haven is now a place of wide open spaces and huge skies with views of the surrounding land that for many centuries in the past could only have been seen by sailors. When we reached Centurion's Copse and walked through the wood again and up the cobbled lane in the hot afternoon sunshine it seemed as if the whole countryside here was asleep. Perhaps it is asleep; so much has happened here in the past that it will have plenty to dream about.

Did you know ?

1   Is it "Centurion", or should it be "St.Urian"?

2   Several unsuccessful attempts were made to reclaim the Haven from the sea, but not until the railway came in 1878 was a permanent dam achieved.

3   The name "Bugle" comes from the Latin "bucullus" meaning a young bull. There are still two inns in the Island carrying this sign, here in Brading and also in Yarmouth. Until recently there was a third, in Newport.

What to look out for

1 Note the remains of cobbles in the lane.

2 Explore Centurion's Copse, a fascinating area, particularly in early summer when the wild flowers are at their best.

3 Look for masses of pink campion and pungent wild garlic.

4 Note the earthworks on the northern side of the Copse.

5 At the Great Sluice, Map Reference 620870, you get your first sight of Brading Haven and can imagine what it must have been like before it was drained.

6 Examine the Great Sluice, and its fine Victorian stonework culvert.

7 As its name implies, Wall Lane, Brading, follows the wall of the old harbour. On the left of the lane you can see where it was - it is now a housing estate.

8 Brading Church must be visited, and especially the Oglander Chapel. Note particularly the Pieta by Michaelangelo.

9 On the way back pause to imagine the Haven full of water, and all manner of sailing ships through the ages, even back to Roman times.

Walking Points

1 Go down the once cobbled path to the Copse, and follow the footpath to the left, to Brading. Map Reference 626867.

2 The wood, on the right, lies open for your exploration, but be warned, parts of it are very boggy and Wellies are really required.

3 Climb the stile at the Great Sluice and the path is very easy to follow along the top of the old embankment.

4 At the other side you come to Wall Lane, and this leads to the Church and the High Street. Suitable for wheel chairs.

5 One of the few walks where the lunch break occurs half way through the walk.

6 Intrepid wheel chairs might survive the cobbled lane down to the Copse, but we cannot really recommend it.

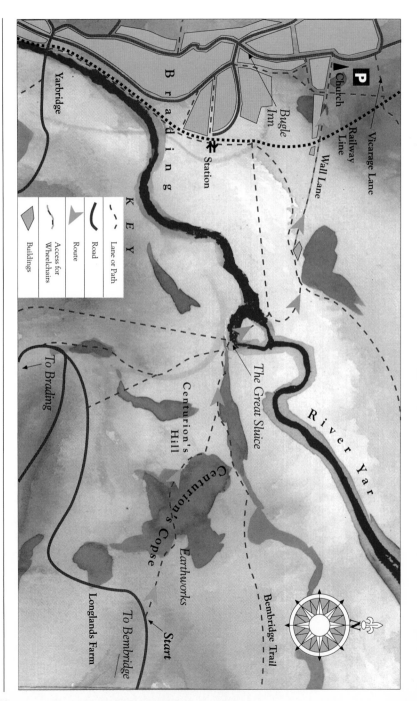

Gallibury Fields

The unexpected pleasure is often the best, and things done on the so-called spur of the moment frequently turn out to be especially attractive. So when at breakfast one morning my wife suddenly said "Shall we drop everything and go for a walk to-day?" I was immediately interested. I looked out of the window. It was October 2nd, the sky was a deep and uninterrupted blue, not a cloud was to be seen, and the faintest of breezes was blowing from a westerly direction. At this time of the year a day such as this was not to be lightly disregarded. It could be a dog day, a day of calm that so often precedes a spell of rainy weather. My mind raced away and I was up on the Downs in Brighstone Forest. It would be wonderful up there this morning, and blissfully peaceful.

My wife read my thoughts. She knows the peculiar fascination this part of the Island has for me, for I frequently talk about it. "I thought we might go and have a look at Gallibury Fields" she said innocently, knowing full well that this was bound to hook me. But why not indeed? We had both planned quite different days, but one of the blessings of retirement is the freedom to change one's mind. What a splendid idea it was that she suggested. "I'll get the maps" I said. "And I'll make the coffee" she replied.

We parked the car at Rowborough Farm on the Bowcombe Road to Shorwell. Rowborough is one of the Domesday manors that the experts cannot agree about for there are two farms of this name in the Island, the other being near Brading. But the truth as to this ancient identification does not really matter, the farmhouse of Rowborough near Shorwell is an old and interesting stone building, looking out down the Bowcombe valley towards Carisbrooke, and it has obviously been there for a long time. God willing, it will be there for many more years to come. Behind it, to the west, the ground rises gradually up Rowborough Bottom with the Downs to the right and Gallibury Fields ahead. The bridleway we intended to take starts here at the farm house (Map Reference 462851) and runs westward along Rowborough Bottom and Fern Bottom for a distance of a mile and a quarter, and then half a mile further on it joins the complex of old roads in Brighstone Forest (Map Reference 434844) which so excite the curiosity, and which we have already written about in the Walk entitled "An Ancient Highway".

The whole area is very hilly with many patches of woodland, and is full of magic and mystery. It is an area of lost villages, reputedly both medieval and pre-Roman, and it is crossed by a network of ancient highways and tracks that no one has really satisfactorily explained. This is possibly why it exercises such a powerful attraction, and of course it is also reasonably remote and can only be visited on foot or on horseback. During the last few years the Isle of Wight has been plagued by several tremendous storms of wind, the first being the great hurricane of October 1987, and many of these high woodland areas suffered great damage. Much has been done to make them suitable for the heavy machinery that was necessary to fell and remove the hundreds of fallen trees. this has inevitably changed the character of the area in places, and there are now several patches of open scrub which once were dense woodland.

As we left the car, shouldering the little pack that contained such essential items as Pat's cameras and

Sloes

the flask of coffee she had prepared, we looked up at the sky. High above us in the clear and central blue were many birds that looked like martins swooping about. Obviously the insects on which they were feeding were flying high this morning, and we both felt that we could not have had a better omen for a continuation of this gorgeous weather. Rowborough farmhouse was being re-roofed, a good sign for its future well-being, and in a field on the right was a row of small breeding houses with triangular roofs covered in blue plastic - not the most environmentally friendly sight - but we took these to be pheasant breeding pens, for we could hear a pheasant calling in the distance. The bridleway was a little muddy to start with, but this soon dried up and within a quarter of a mile, by the time we were entering the woods it was grassed over which made walking very pleasant. The verges of the track were densely lined with nettles, said to be a sign of previous human presence, and along the track itself was an almost continuous border of the large daisy-like Mayweed.

Fern Bottom, with the dark mass of Brighstone Forest showing beyond.

There were many other late wild flowers still to be seen including scabious, vetch, ragwort, thistles, and great banks of teasels, long since withered but still standing erect and proud. The trees on the edge of the wood were mainly sycamores, and on the other side of the bridleway a hedge of cobnuts with here and there a sloe, both the latter bearing fruit. Occasionally there were little clumps of mushrooms and other fungi, and many dandelion type flowers dotted about. We took these to be either hawkweed or hawksbeard of which

there are several varieties, but unfortunately we are not by any means expert botanists - we simply love the flowers we see and like to identify them.

At the end of this woodland path, almost a mile from our starting point, we came to a five barred gate and a stile. This marked the end of Rowborough Bottom and the beginning of Fern Bottom, and from this junction (Map Reference 449847) a third valley went off at right angles called Bunkers Bottom. But the sight we had been waiting to see was the great bulk of Gallibury Fields towering away to our right. This huge natural spur rises steeply from the 50 metre contour in Fern Bottom to 200 metres at the top less than half a mile away. This is impressive at any time, but to-day, bathed in bright sunshine and with a perfectly blue sky above it, it was magnificent. We sat on the stile and drank our coffee, preparing ourselves for the climb to the top which we knew would be tiring. A number of sheep were grazing on the hillside and these added a further dimension to the beauty of the scene.

There are two theories about the meaning of the name "Gallibury". One is that it simply means "the fortified place of the Gaels", and the other that it is a gallows hill. Both are probably correct. As we slowly climbed

Track through Lower Kingate Copse, Rowborough Bottom. Splendid going underfoot.

the hill - for this type of exercise is not one of our favourites and we had to stop several times to rest - we thought about both these meanings, and also how fit the people of those far off times must have been. As we paused we turned round to look at the view that was steadily unfolding below us, and this view alone made climbing the hill worthwhile.

Eastwards we looked right across the Island and in the far distance could see the white gleam of Culver Cliff. Slightly south of east was the immensely tall T.V. mast on Chillerton Down, and between us and these landmarks, and indeed all around, was the most glorious panorama of Island scenery, enough to gladden anyone's heart. Westwards the scene was quite different, for close at hand, less than half a mile away, was the great spread of Brighstone Forest, a mass of undulating woodland at a similar level to Gallibury itself. But it was an item due south of us that really caught our imagination. On the other side of Fern Bottom is Cheverton Down, and immediately below us on the lower slopes of this Down was an area in which there was a number of humps and banks, the shadows of which were clearly visible to the naked eye from our lofty vantage point. Could this be one of the lost Bronze Age villages dating back about 3000 years? One group of banks clearly marked a square enclosure, and of course it is known that these primitive people did build animal pounds with earthwork walls. This was indeed an exciting possibility.

We clambered on, refreshed in spirit if not in body, and as we neared the top we came to the remains of the earthwork which these ancient people had constructed as a defensive measure. This great bank must have originally enclosed a very large area of several acres and we were surprised to find that it had recently been ploughed following the taking of a crop, for there was a rim of stubble round the field. The soil looked of very poor quality, absolutely riddled with flints, indeed there were more flints that there was earth, and the yield to the farmer must have been very disap-

pointing. As we walked along we could not resist searching for flints, for even the remote possibility of finding something interesting was compelling.

Pat found several small flints with very sharp edges that could easily have served as scrapers or saws, but the most intriguing one she picked up was half a round stone two and a half inches in diameter. This had been cleanly severed and the half she found had a smooth rim about half an inch wide in the shape of a horsehoe. But it was the interior of the flint that literally caught the eye for it sparkled with a myriad minute pin points of light, so it must presumably have been a piece of quartz or something similar. We brought this away with us and it sits on my desk as I write, glinting away with every slightest movement of my head.

This magical spot on the top of Gallibury Fields not only marked the apex of our walk but also the point at which we had to think about getting back for we had spent far more time dillying and dallying than we had intended. The quickest way would have been to retrace our steps but we rejected this option as we like all our walks to take a circular route. We contemplated taking a short cut across Bunkers Bottom to get back into the wood on Rowborough Down but decided this would not be a good idea for we knew what it involved. Bunkers Bottom is a grassy valley and apart from the steepness of its sides it provides very good walking, but on the other side of it is a very rough piece of ground indeed and we had been caught in this before now. Rowborough Down is well named, for the first element of the word, "row" means "rough".

*Rosebay
Willowherb*

Across the ploughed field on the top of Gallibury we could see a gate into the wood, and we knew that his would lead us to the very same ancient highway that we have previously mentioned and from which we could get back on well defined forest tracks to Rowborough Farm. We have learned the wisdom of keeping to these established footpaths, for to stray from them

Checking the map, Fern Bottom. Gallibury Fields is on the top of the hill, to the left.

brings the risk of getting lost or at least finding yourself in very difficult terrain. So please do heed this friendly warning and stick to the footpaths or bridleways, there are plenty of them. The forest is a wonderful place but it is large and wild and can show you a sinister side if you trifle with it.

We had a truly delightful walk back through the woods on tracks that were mostly grassy and springy underfoot. Evidence of storm damage was only too apparent in places, but where the trees had gone the sunlight was able to get through and already the wild flowers had established themselves. In the open spaces along the way we found heather, self heal, viper's bugloss and marjoram, and several others that we could not name. There were butterflies too, speckled browns, red admirals, and tortoiseshells, and in the woods rabbits and many pheasants. Another plant we could not help but notice was our favourite Travellers Joy which was now quite over and in seed. We wished we had been here a few weeks ago for there was masses of it and it must have been a magnificent sight when in full bloom.

The next, and penultimate, part of our walk was difficult. We were coming down from the wood into Rowborough Bottom on to the bridle way on which we had set out. It was only a few hundred yards down a deeply rutted chalk road but it was steep and most uncomfortable to the feet. There were compensations however, the chalk was blinding white in the strong

sunshine and this seemed to make the blue of the sky even deeper in colour. Down one side of this chalk lane was a hedge composed largely of dogwood whose heaves were already turned to a delightful shade of dark red. Once down on the level we went past the pheasant breeding pens and were soon back at the car, tired but very satisfied with where we had been and what we had seen. We were also very hungry and it was now nearly 2.30.

And then I had a brainwave. Before Pat suggested this walk on the spur of the moment she had been planning a visit to the supermarket in Newport to buy fruit. As a matter of principle we are not keen on supermarkets for they have been the death of many a local trader, and much of the money they take does not stay on the Island but goes to the mainland. But the services they provide and the range of goods carried is truly admirable, and this particular supermarket in Newport has the best selection of fresh fruit and vegetables I have ever seen. Also it has a cafeteria, and I remembered that this provides hot food all through the day. This struck us both as being an undoubted attraction at the present moment, so this is where we went. It was good to sit down and have something to eat, and afterwards we were able to buy our fruit. We left the supermarket car park well satisfied with a very satisfactory conclusion to an extremely happy outing.

Did you know ?

1   Rowborough Bottom and Down are both full of wild flowers - scabious, ragwort, vetches, thistles, great banks of teasels, hawkweed or hawksbeard, plants of the dandelion family, self heal, vipers bugloss, marjoram, and travellers joy. The latter in abundance in season.

2   In October the dogwood was turning red, both cobnuts and sloes were fruiting, and there were many butterflies about - speckled browns, red admirals and tortoiseshells.

Total Distance Walked : 3 miles

What to look out for

1   From Rowborough Farm it is a pleasant walk of almost a mile up Rowborough Bottom to Fern Bottom and the first sight of Gallibury Fields, towering away on your right.

2   Note the pheasant breeding pens on the right near the Farm.

3   Note the bank of willow herb on the side of Rowborough Down and their thistledown type seed heads in autumn.

4   A very steep climb to the top of Gallibury Fields, but well worth it when you get there. Note the ancient earthwork on the top.

5   Landmarks that can be seen from the top of Gallibury .

Chillerton T.V. mast to the south east, Culver Cliff to the east, and Brighstone Forest to the west. Admire the view while you get your breath back.

6   Look down on the "lost" village on the other side of Fern Bottom. Our picture shows part of this.

7   Note Bunkers Bottom, a beautiful grassy valley to the east.

Walking Points

1   Follow the bridleway from Rowborough Farm up Rowborough Bottom. First part is very muddy after rain but most of it is grassed over and is pleasant to walk on.

2   At the end of Rowborough Bottom climb or open the gate into Fern Bottom.

3   After climbing up to Gallibury Fields follow the path round the ploughed field to a gate into the wood. In the wood turn right on to a woodland track leading eastwards to Rowborough-down Bottom.

4   There are several woodland tracks here, all of which will lead ultimately back to Rowborough Farm.

5   Resist the temptation to leave the established paths, for between them the terrain is very rough. But these woodland tracks make for easy walking and are delightful.

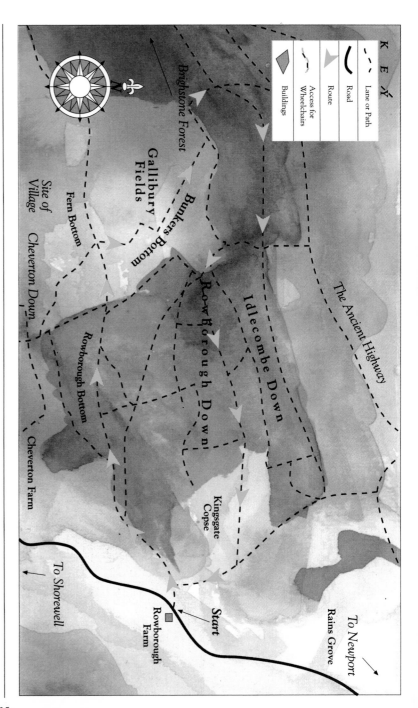

The End of the Line

hey say that walking is good for you, and no one would really dispute this. Unfortunately, although you may desperately want to get out into the open and go striding over the Downs this is not always possible. Health and physique may preclude you from striding anywhere very much, illness may lay you low, and even if you are fit there are so many distractions and complications in this world of ours towards the end of the 20th century that the days and the weeks fly by with ever increasing rapidity. Sometimes you begin to despair, and wonder whether you will ever get going again.

So that after a long enforced spell of inactivity, when the opportunity to break out does ultimately arise, it gives you a grand and glorious feeling of release. A sort of 'end of-term' feeling, a feeling that in the Army was described as being 'de-mob happy'. And you jump at it with open arms and a thankful heart. It does not really matter very much where you go, the great thing is to get up and go somewhere, to get out into the open, to get away from main roads and motor cars, to breathe the clean sea air, and to thank God for the Isle of Wight.

February is often a rotten month weather-wise in this country, but even the weather is not all that important providing you have adequate clothing to keep you dry and warm. But when a day that promises to be warm and sunny comes along there is additional reason to be joyful, and it was on just such a day in February that we were able to enjoy the walk we now want to share with you. Unfortunately, the promise of sunshine was not fulfilled, and by the time we started the skies had clouded over. But never mind. Even on a grey day the walk was delightful.

This walk is an old favourite of ours and one we have done in all sorts of weather conditions ranging from the bleak mid-winter to the boiling hot days of summer. Basically it involves walking from Yarmouth to Freshwater, and then by a different route from Freshwater back to Yarmouth, a circular trip along both banks of the river Yar, and covering in all about 5 miles. The outward journey was entirely on the flat since the route lay along the track of the dismantled Freshwater, Yarmouth and Newport Railway, one of the most delightfully scenic of all the old Island railways that were abolished in the 1950's because they were uneconomic. But what a splendid tourist attraction this railway line would have been to-day had it still been running, for indeed all the way from the West Wight right into Newport the scenery is charming. However, it is an ill wind that blows no-one any good, and the railways loss is our gain.

We left the car at Yarmouth Station, (Map Ref. 358894) almost alongside the platform that is still there, the station building itself now being a Youth Club and Community Centre. Coming down off the platform on to what was the line we turned towards the river. In front of us was Yarmouth Mill, a rather gaunt rectangular building, now a holiday home. The mill was built in 1793 by William Porter, a Newport hawker turned builder who could neither read nor write. He relied on a local Bank to keep his books for him, and when the Bank failed in 1794 poor old William found that he too was ruined. None of his friends turned to help him and he died in poverty.

The railway line bends to the left and for the next half mile or so follows the river closely, separated only by great swathes of reeds. On the left is Thorley Marsh,

Alder Catkins

a large expanse of marshland that many centuries ago was in fact Yarmouth's harbour, known as the Drafthaven. This harbour, long before Yarmouth breakwater was built, was capable of receiving quite large ships, but it gradually silted up and became useless, and the building of a dam across its entrance and the construction of the first mill in 1663 finally sealed it from the sea. The marsh is very low lying and prone to flooding, and to-day there was a lot of water about. There were many waders and sea birds to be spotted, and we counted one flock of over 30 teal. We passed several people with binoculars watching the birds, and I have no doubt that the birds were equally vigilant in watching the humans.

Yarmouth Mill, built in 1793 but now a holiday home.

Some years ago the authorities surfaced the old railway track with stone chippings, making walking rather uncomfortable, but this has now been well trampled down and amalgamated with mother earth, and the surface is quite smooth and dry. The views as we walked this straight section of the track were rewarding, relaxing and highly satisfactory. On our left the marsh, bounded by Mill Copse and Thorley Copse, ahead of us the track which soon became flanked by bramble and hawthorn hedges, and on our right reed beds and river.

Although it is 40 years since the railway closed there are still traces of the old line to be seen, one or two concrete posts and the remains of the post and wire fence that bordered the track. A little further on across

the river we could see Kings Manor, one of the Island's most beautiful old houses. At the time of the Domesday Survey in 1086 this was the most important manor in the Freshwater area, though the whole district belonged either to the King or to the Prior of Christchurch. The house was looking rather grey and sombre to-day and though we waited for some time for a photograph in the hope of a little sunshine there were too many clouds about.

Thirty years ago some rebuilding of Kings Manor was carried out in stone from the demolished Ventnor Hospital, and this may have contributed to its rather grey appearance, but sitting on the bank of the river it is in a most attractive setting, 'far from the madding crowd'. Earlier this century Queen Mary, who frequently came to Yarmouth, paid a visit to Kings, arriving by boat at their private landing stage. On the landing stage she found a notice saying 'Kings Only', and the Queen is reputed to have commented on this, expressing the hope that she would not be turned away.

Opposite Kings Manor the railway line passes through some rather scruffy woodland, fringed on the river side by reed beds. In the woods were many clumps of

The railway track to Freshwater.

98

yellow bog Iris, still festooned with bright orange berries, also some fern and much 'mother-in-law's tongue', the latter being a rather surprising find. A robin burst into song as we passed, no doubt as a warning to us that we were trespassing on his territory, and reminding us that it will not be long now before the robins start mating. Already in our garden on fine days there is much bird activity, with the blue tits and great tits beginning to take an interest in the nesting boxes, and our resident robin has already allowed another to come into his territory, a sure sign that there is something in the wind.

Beyond the woodland the river bends to the right and the railway track faithfully follows suit. Once clear of the wood there is an open space on which a thoughtful council have erected a seat. Here we sat down and drank our coffee, revelling in the peace and placid beauty of the scene before us. The tide was high, which is the best time to see this part of the river, and on the other side of this wide and still sheet of water the ground rises quickly up to Freshwater Church. Dedicated to All Saints, this church is one of the oldest in the Island and was founded soon after the coming of Christianity to the Isle of Wight in 686. Little trace is left now of the first Saxon church, for the village of Freshwater has grown in size and the church has been extended and rebuilt to keep pace with this growth, but the present building is a beautiful and typical village church.

A few yards further on we came to The Causeway, a road crossing the railway line and river, and marking the end of the open tidal water. On the left of the track is a charming little cottage which, when the railway was working, was the level crossing keeper's cottage, and on the river were two swans and many sea birds.

The track continues across the road through thick beds of reeds, curving steadily to the right and culminating in what was Freshwater Station. In the place of the station now is a small cafe-cum-restaurant called -

appropriately - The End of the Line, and this is a place we know well for it specialises in home-made food at very reasonable prices. Particularly to be recommended are their Quiches and Apple Pie, and they produce the most interesting salads we know of in this part of the world. The End of the Line is understandably popular and we were grateful to find an empty table for two. By the time we left we were refreshed and fortified, and looking forward to the return trip down the other side of the river.

At the back of the cafe is a garden centre and other buildings all erected on what was once Freshwater Station and Sidings - literally the end of the line. Round the corner of these buildings we walked and found ourselves at the bottom of Hooke Hill leading up to the oldest part of Freshwater and the Church. Hooke Hill commemorates Robert Hooke, one of the most extraordinary men the Isle of Wight has ever produced. He was born here in Freshwater on 18th July 1635, his father being the Rector. As a child he was physically weak and puny but was possessed of a massive brain, and when he grew up he became one of the leading philosophers and scientists of the age, a friend of Christopher Wren, Isaac Newton and many other famous men. He was a founder of the Royal Society and its first Secretary. Under his guidance, and the patronage of Charles II, the Society achieved an international reputation for furthering scientific research, and Hooke continued his work right up until his death in March 1702. At the bottom of the hill there is a stone plinth bearing a plaque in his honour, and describing him simply as 'Physicist, Scientist, Architect, and Inventor'.

All Saints Church, of which Robert Hooke's father was Rector, later became associated with another famous man, for it was at this church that Alfred Lord Tennyson, the Poet Laureate, worshipped when he was living at nearby Farringford. There are several reminders of Tennyson in the Church, including two stained glass windows created by his friends the

Beech Leaves and Harestail Grass

painters George Frederick Watts and Hollman Hunt. Tennyson is of course buried in Poets Corner in Westminster Abbey, but Lady Tennyson's grave is here in the churchyard. From the Church a footpath points the way to Yarmouth across the fields and this provides a very pleasant walk of just over 2 miles. The river is never very far from sight and most of the time you look down on it from the high ground, the views across it to the rolling country beyond being well worth pausing to see.

The Memorial to Robert Hooke, one of Freshwater's most famous sons.

Just over half a mile from the Church the footpath takes you past the gateway, and cattle grid, to Kings Manor, and after nearly another half mile the ground drops temporarily to a little brook which is on its way to join the river. Here there are two stiles and a footbridge over the stream surrounded by a few trees, a very attractive little corner. A footpath from Norton Green joins the route here, Norton being one of the five districts into which Freshwater was once divided. The others are Easton, Weston, Middleton, and Sutton. Once over the footbridge the ground rises again, and not until you reach Saltern Wood and are nearing the end of the walk does the path finally plunge down through the trees to the river valley and Yarmouth Harbour.

The last three quarters of a mile or so is of absorbing interest to anyone who has a liking for water, for an estuary, for a harbour, and for small boats. As we approached the harbour there were many wild geese and other sea birds to be photographed, and the harbour itself is always colourful and interesting. Over the new bridge we walked, with yachts of all shapes and sizes to left and to right of us. The Yarmouth Lifeboat, which is often in the news, was moored just off the Quay, and as we walked into the town a Ferry was leaving for Lymington, the mainland shore being faintly visible in the mist a couple of miles or so away.

Feeling the need for a cup of tea we went into the Square and looked up at the Church clock. It was actually half past three, but inevitably we thought of Rupert Brooke.

"Stands the church clock at ten to three?
And is there honey still for tea?"

In Barnacles Restaurant in Bridge Road, next door to the very house we owned when we first came to Yarmouth, there was no honey on the menu, but we succumbed to their special cream tea, which was excellent, and which we felt we had earned. Then a visit to the Church which we knew so well, just to pay our respects and say thank you for everything, and then tired but very content along Mill Road to the Mill and back to the car.

Total Distance Walked: 5 miles

Did you know ?

1. Yarmouth is the oldest town in the Island. It was built as a town on the grid system in the 12th century.

2. Yarmouth Mill, built in 1793 by William Porter who could neither read nor write.

3. Lady Tennyson is buried in Freshwater churchyard, but her husband lies in Poets Corner in Westminster Abbey.

4. The River Yar between Yarmouth and Freshwater is fringed with reed beds and many other marsh plants. Kingfishers may sometimes be seen.

What to look out for

1 Note Yarmouth Station and platform left practically unchanged, but still usefully employed.

2 The old railway track runs alongside the river, and on the left is Thorley Marsh which before it silted up was the Drafthaven capable of taking large sea-going ships.

3 See how many waders and sea birds you can see on river and marsh.

4 Kings Manor on the opposite bank of the river, an elegant old house with a history going back to Domesday. Note the Causeway and Railway Crossing Keeper's cottage.

5 The End of the Line, a cafe-restaurant on the site of Freshwater Station.

6 The Robert Hooke Memorial. Hooke, a founder and secretary of the Royal Society, was born in Freshwater, son of the Rector.

7 Visit the Church. Stained glass Tennyson windows by G.F. Watts and Holman Hunt. Representations of Lady Tennyson and Ellen Terry.

8 Back in Yarmouth also visit the Church, one of the most peaceful in the Isle of Wight.

Walking Points

1 Yarmouth is readily accessible by bus from Newport, or you can park a car in the old station yard.

2 Walk down the ramp at the end of the old platform and leave Yarmouth Mill on your right, the distance from Freshwater being just over 1.1/2 miles. Wheel chairs start from Mill Road.

3 Walking surface is hard and dry but a bit rough on the feet. Follow the railway track literally to the End of the Line.

4 Coming back go up Hooke Hill to the Church, past the Hooke Memorial. The footpath to Yarmouth skirts the churchyard to the left.

5 The footpath is well marked all the way and beings you to the western side of Yarmouth Harbour. There are several stiles.

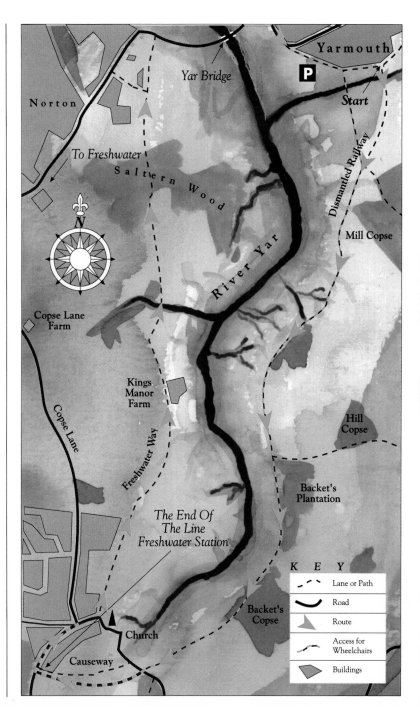

A Short Walk to the Longstone

The winter had not been severe, and though there had been many grey days, some wind, rain and fog, it was only on a few occasions that the bird bath had become frozen overnight. Nevertheless, when March came around, and the spring began to manifest itself, we experienced a great surge of hope and anticipation with the knowledge that soon we would be able to realise some of the dreams we had dreamed during the dark days. For who does not dream, during the winter of getting out into the open air again away from all the stresses and petty niggles of life?

For me personally there is one part of the Island that consistently calls, a part to which I feel irresistably drawn and of which I never tire, no matter how many visits we make. Very approximately, this is the downland area of the West Wight, the highlights of which are Rowborough Down, Brighstone Down, and Mottistone Down, though I am reluctant to omit from this short list such fascinating uplands as Bowcombe Down, Westridge Down, Cheverton Down, and Afton Down. Etcetera, etcetera. Perhaps it would be safer to say that the area that particularly attracts me is the whole of the West Wight! There is something about this part of the Island, a feeling of tranquillity and peace, perhaps born of its long, long history - for the uplands were known to man in neolithic times - that brings great comfort and relaxation to these jaded years at the end of the 20th century.

One early day in March we woke to find the sun shining in a cloudless sky, and though we had seen other mornings like this in which the promise of a fine day had not been fulfilled, we had a feeling that on this particular day the sunshine was going to last. At breakfast we discussed the possibility of dropping everything we had planned to do, and agreed that as this might prove to be a dog day - that is, a perfect day sandwiched in the middle of a spell of cloudy and misty weather - it would be foolish to miss the opportunity. Our judgement on this occasion was correct, the weather did hold for the day, and by breakfast time the following morning it was raining.

Where to go? I fetched a map. Perhaps the route we chose was not an entirely suitable one for the first expedition for some time. We should perhaps have chosen a flatter and less tiring walk than the one we picked on, for though it was short it admittedly had its steep and hilly bits and was a bit hard on the legs. But oh what a glorious walk it turned out to be!

Basically, as a first objective we decided to visit the Longstone at Mottistone, which my wife had long been itching to photograph in the sunshine with a blue sky behind it. The only pictures we had were taken in the days when the stones were surrounded by trees, but now the trees were gone the whole area had a different look to it, and it was possible to photograph the stones from any angle.

The hurricane that hit the South of England so ferociously in October 1987 did an unbelievable amount of damage in this area, and even to-day almost five years later, tidying up work is still going on. We left the car in Strawberry Lane near Brighstone at the beginning of Footpath No.85. (Map Reference 412837) and even before we started to walk we could hear the chain saws buzzing away in the woods. At one time this was a thickly wooded path snaking up the side of Castle Hill, but now the trees have thinned out and it

Daisy

was not long before we emerged into the sunlight. The views as we climbed higher up the hill became increasingly interesting and because the trees were now gone we could see the sea below, and away to the west Highdown Cliffs. Beyond Highdown in the far distance we could just make out the cliffs of the mainland near St.Alban's Head. Immediately down below us were the roofs of Mottistone Manor and the village church.

Highdown Cliffs from Mottistone Common.

But the hillside on which we were standing showed only too clearly the devastation caused by the storm. Not a tree to be seen over a band several hundred yards wide, but the whole hillside beautifully planted out with hundreds of new trees. The task facing the Forestry Commission must have been daunting, and full marks must be given to them for the way in which they cleared the site and started again. The strange course taken by the hurricane could also be seen, for after mowing down this wide swathe of timber on Mottistone Common and Castle Hill it went on to cut a similar swathe through Grammar's Common to the east, before then continuing its attack on into Brighstone Forest where we had already seen the damage caused.

The only thing the storm had failed to flatten was the Longstone itself which still stands unscathed as it has done for close on 5000 years. Strangely enough, now the two stones are out in the open they are not as impressive as they were when surrounded by trees. Somehow some of the mystery and the aura of antiquity has left them and they look smaller than before. However, they are still impressive enough and their setting is idyllic with huge vistas to north and east, and the sea to the south. What a wonderful spot those ancient people chose in which to erect their monument.

Not far from the Longstone is a bench seat, and here we sat, protected by a fold in the ground from the chill breeze that was blowing, and drank our coffee, marvelling in the view before us and thankful for the ability and opportunity that this glorious day had provided. Pat then got to work with her cameras, prowling round the stones and examining them from every angle. They are said to be of local origin, and one can only wonder at the enormous labour involved in bringing them even a short distance and erecting them in this remote spot. The surface of the stones is very curious, weather beaten of course, and full of delicate colours in shades of yellow, red, and green.

View from the Longstone towards Strawberry Lane, Brighstone Forest behind.

The Longstone is the oldest relic of antiquity in the Island, and originally the two stones are thought to have been erected vertically, a few inches apart, marking the eastern end of a 70 foot long barrow which was a communal burial chamber. They were so orientated that at dawn on the day of the winter solstice the sun's rays would shine between them straight down the whole length of the tomb, and by so doing awaken the spirits of the dead. The ability of an ancient people to carry out such a precise building operation can to-day only make us marvel. The date is believed to have been around 3500 B.C., give or take a few hundred years.

The Neolithic Age, or New Stone Age, as this period in our history is known, was followed after 2000 years by the Bronze Age, and after another period of about a thousand years by the Iron Age. After yet another spell of around 750 years the modern method of numbering the years began with the birth of Jesus Christ. The B.C. period (Before Christ) came to an end and men began counting again from A.D.1, Anno Domini, the year of Our Lord. The world has now managed to stagger through nearly two thousand of these years, which means that the Longstones have been around for a very considerable time. They were already very old in the Bronze Age, and the men who lived in the Island at that time venerated the stones, though possibly having no idea of their original significance, but used them as a communal focal point, a meeting place. From the name they gave them - the Meeting Stones - sprang the name of the village that grew up nearby, Mottistone.

We roused ourselves from thoughts of the past and continued the walk, revelling in the sunshine and the blue sky. The path we followed took us through the edge of the wood, now making steadily northwards towards the great mass of Mottistone Down. On our right in the huge bowl of the valley a ploughman in his tractor was methodically ploughing long straight furrows from one side to the other, deftly turning his plough at the rim of the bowl on each side rather like a skateboarder in slow motion. Gradually as he traversed back and forth the straw coloured ground was turned to a rich dark brown, and a flock of seagulls patiently followed the plough.

As we reached the lower slopes of the Down we found ahead of us a long disused chalk pit now overgrown with vegetation and many small trees. Then began the steepest part of the walk with a climb up to the top of the Down. Here the turf was soft and springy with occasional clumps of gorse, some of which were already bursting into flower, and there were obviously many, many rabbits frequenting the hillside. Pausing every few yards to rest and admire the view we watched the ploughman down below finish his task as the last pale strip of land disappeared under the plough.

At the top the view was breathtaking and you really felt you were on top of the world. Here we came to a track, one of the oldest of the many ancient highways to be found in the Island, a road whose origins go back probably to the days of the Longstone itself. This road is described in the chapter on Ancient Highways in 'The Enchanted Isle', as it has long fascinated me, and it was this way we now took, heading eastwards. The going underfoot was excellent, a soft and close cropped turf and mercifully downhill, which after the climb up on to the Down was a great blessing. We swung along this green and pleasant way with renewed energy, and both found ourselves chuckling with the sheer delight of being alive and able to enjoy this magical place.

The slope led gently downhill for half a mile, and at the bottom is the National Trust Car park alongside the main Calbourne to Brighstone road (Map Reference 420845). As we neared the car park a van disgorged a number of small boys with mountain bikes who set off pedalling furiously up the hill we were descending, though the smallest little fellow was actually pushing his bike but bravely trying to keep up with the rest. Apart from the fact that in their excitement they forgot to close the gate leading out of the car

Ploughing near the Longstone. The devastation round the Stones can be seen very clearly.

tucked into the hillside close to a disused chalk pit, one of many in the area. In less than a mile's walk down this very pleasant country lane, which has no white lines, no yellow lines, nor any sign of man's desecration, we were back at the car and ready for our lunch. Being lucky enough to have a car we had a choice of local pubs, the Sun at Calbourne, the Three Bishops at Brighstone, the Sun at Hulverstone, or the Crown at Shorwell, at all of which we knew we could get good food. We chose the Crown, but as it was well after two o'clock we wondered what sort of a reception we should receive when asking for food.

We need not have worried. We went into the bar and I asked mine host if we were too late for something to eat. "Of course not" he said cheerfully "You are most welcome". And somehow this set the seal on our very pleasant expedition. We sat down gratefully with a drink and discussed the walk. We had seen very few wild flowers, a few dandelions and daisies mainly, and surprisingly one sprig of pink campion. The most striking feature of the walk was the enormous amount of tree planting that the Forestry Commission had achieved. It really made you feel that the Island was in good hands.

We had a splendid meal finishing off with treacle tart and cream, a long time favourite of mine, and coffee. But it was really the welcome we received at the Crown which brought everything to such a satisfactory conclusion.

park they were well behaved and probably getting as much enjoyment out of their surroundings as we were. It was good to see them.

Our way did not lie along the main road but back down Strawberry Lane which joins it at this point. Not far from here is the site of the Roman Villa at Rock overlooking the great valley down which Strawberry Lane plunged. Half way down we stopped to look at an old lime kiln, long since defunct. This kiln is

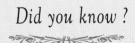

Did you know ?

On the top of Mottistone Down you are on the same ancient highway we have walked before (See 'An Ancient Highway'). Looking east you can see this track snaking along the edge of Brighstone Forest.

Primrose

Total Distance Walked: 3.5 miles.

What to look out for

1   The views from the cleared woodland on FP85 are excellent. On a clear day you can see St. Albans Head.

2   Look down from FP85 and see Mottistone Manor and the village church

3   Note the neat but unobtrusive re-planting of trees as you ascend the track.

4   The Longstone. Two stones in fact, one vertical, one horizontal. When erected 5000 years ago they were both vertical.

5   As you walk from the Longstone to Mottistone Down note the disused chalk pit on your left, a typical feature of this chalk downland country.

6   On top of Mottistone Down there are more stunning views, but you have a bit of a climb to get there.

7   Plenty of gorse up here in Spring, and rabbits all the year round.

8   Have a look at the valley as you descend Strawberry Lane. Up here was Rock Roman Villa with a typical beautiful vista.

9   Note the old lime kiln halfway down Strawberry Lane.

Walking Points

1   Plenty of room to park at the beginning of FP85 at Map Reference 413837.

2   Starting up FP85 the going underfoot is good all the way to the Stones.

3   On the next stretch, crossing the valley to the foot of Mottistone Down, there can be some muddy patches after rain.

4   The climb up the down is short but steep, but rewarding. The turf is soft and springy.

5   From the top it is gently downhill all the way to the National Trust Car Park where you turn sharp right into Strawberry Lane.

6   FP85 and Strawberry Lane are hilly, but should both be negotiable by wheel chairs.

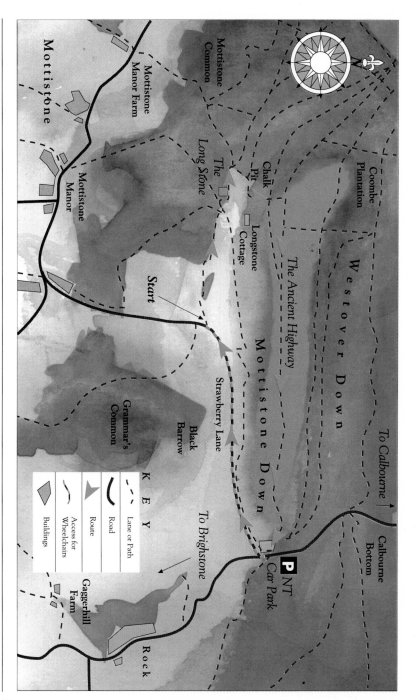

Hamstead

The name Hamstead is Anglo-Saxon and means simply a "homestead". Even to-day, possibly 1200 years since the original homestead was built, there are still very few buildings in the area, which is truly rural and excellent walking country. Hamstead is first mentioned in the Domesday Survey, half of it having been given by the Norman Lord of the Island to his henchman William FitzStur, and the other half to William's younger brother Gozelin. 200 years later the FitzSturs were no longer in possession of the whole of the estate, part of it being listed in 1284 as belonging to Quarr Abbey and the other part to the Priory of Christchurch.

To-day the Hamstead Estate is privately owned, but there is a network of public footpaths which make it possible for all of us to enjoy this delightful and secluded corner of the Isle of Wight. There is good walking here at any time of the year, for it is not too hilly, the going underfoot is good, and there are many splendid views to enjoy, over both countryside and sea. One summer's day we decided to go this way, for though the day promised to be hot we knew that walking through the woods would be delightful, and that once we reached the cliffs at Hamstead there was sure to be a breeze to cool us down.

We began at Ningwood Common, via Hamstead Road, an un-made road that leaves the A3054 Newport to Yarmouth road at Map Ref.: 394893. This is a pleasant road to walk along, but we actually took the car about half a mile or so up the road and left it near the junction with Solent Road, at 398901. This shortened the walk by about a mile and still left us with around 3.75 miles to cover on foot. We regard four miles as being about our maximum, but if you want a longer walk then leave the car at the beginning of Hamstead Road. You can of course reach this spot readily by bus, for there is a good service from Newport to Yarmouth.

From the junction mentioned above (398901) we were on the estate' roads proper, and after only a quarter of a mile through the woods reached Pigeon Coo Farm which is delightfully situated at a junction of woodland roads. Not only delightfully situated, but delightfully named too, and indicative of the bird life that abounds in these woods. The sun was shining through the trees from a cloudless blue sky, but it was still cool and pleasant for walking, and already we were beginning to feel away from it all. We always experience this feeling of having reached a haven as we approach Hamstead, for this is an area that holds for us many happy memories.

Soon after passing Pigeon Coo Farm the track forks to the right but we kept straight on heading due north, for we intended in fact to come back by the other track. Soon the wood came to an end and we were out in the open, the sun streaming down from a clear blue sky. On our left we passed piggeries which suffered a sad and cruel blow in 1981 when Hamstead was hit by a savage, though mercifully isolated, attack of foot and mouth disease when the farm's entire stock of cattle and pigs had to be slaughtered and burned. At the time it seemed a terrible and tragic waste, but it was obviously the right thing to do for the outbreak was contained and never spread to the rest of the Island.

Though this is not a hilly walk the ground rises steadily up to Hamstead Grange which is the manor house. Just before reaching the gates leading into the

Wild Parsley

109

drive the view to the right stopped us in our tracks for here you can look down on the estuary of the Newtown River and beyond it up the Solent all the way to Gurnard and Cowes. This is a superb vista which in the 1960's came within an ace of being lost for ever.

A proposal was put forward to build a nuclear power station on this spot because of the ample water available for cooling purposes, and one can only shudder at the thought of the desecration this would have caused to the environment. Fortunately, the Island's leading resident, Lord Mottistone, conducted a vigorous campaign against the scheme in both Houses of Parliament, printing and distributing leaflets to all members. He had on his side a powerful economic argument, namely the cost of conveying the generated electricity back to the mainland, and the plan was ultimately dropped.

Newtown River estuary, looking across to Clamerkin. It was here that a Nuclear Power Station was proposed.

The present Hamstead Grange is not of great age, but is a comfortable late Victorian house, though its site is of course very much older. When it was an ecclesiastical holding it was for centuries a true grange, or granary for the monastery that owned it, and later in 1806 the estate was bought by the celebrated architect John Nash who redesigned and rebuilt the dilapidated old house he found here. This he used as a shooting box, his principal residence in the Island being East Cowes Castle which he built at about the same time. Nash also founded a brickworks at Lower Hamstead, serviced by a light railway, and encouraged salt production in the local salterns. Sadly, all traces of the brickworks and the railway have now disappeared,

and even Nash's house itself became so dilapidated that it had to be demolished during the second world war.

At the entrance to the grounds of Hamstead Grange the public right of way swerves to the left and goes right round the gardens and through the farm buildings behind. Here on the left is a pleasant modern house built on the site of John Nash's Shooting Box, and after passing this and going through a farm gate the lane leads in a north-easterly direction straight for the sea, barely quarter of a mile away. The cliffs here are not very high, are shelving, and subject to erosion, but have a great scientific reputation, being rich in fossils. Once there was a grove of pine trees on the top of the cliffs, but storms and erosion have taken their toll and the view of the sea is now much more open.

We were right about the cooling breeze, which was most welcome, and we looked upon a very satisfying

The celtic cross memorial commemorating three sad deaths by drowning in these treacherous waters.

scene of blue sea and sky with the mainland about three miles away across the water. Several white hulled and white sailed yachts plying the peaceful waters below added to the tranquillity of the picture.

Just to our left, jutting out from the shore, were the remains of a war-time boom, designed to keep enemy ships out of the Solent and Spithead, but not much of this is now left. The sea below us looked calm and peaceful enough, but this is a treacherous stretch of water and sailors of small boats have to beware. Hamstead Ledge is a notorious shingle bank stretching out under water in a north-westerly direction, and on a spring ebb the water boils up from below in furious fashion, creating a vicious sea that has cost several boat owners their lives.

One such tragedy occurred in 1864 when Teresa Farnall, a 19 year old local girl, together with her younger brother, was being taken for a sail in a 12 foot dinghy by her boy friend. The tide turned while they were out and a strong ebb began to run. Crossing the rough water over the ledge they capsized and the girl was drowned. We were musing on this sad accident as the path took us down from the cliff on to a grassy way at the back of the beach, and here we found a memorial to yet another small boat tragedy.

This memorial, in the form of a Celtic cross commemorates the deaths of three young men on two separate occasions. The first one was in November 1932 when both David Cox and his friend William Pollock aged 20 were drowned when their boat foundered, and the second one remembers Robin Cox who was lost in June 1934 when aged 21. Were David and Robin brothers, we wondered, and was this memorial erected by their sorrowing parents?

These rather sad thoughts were perhaps in keeping with the place, for the official guide to this part of the coast says it is inadvisable to leave the path hereabouts for even in summer the ground is very soft and it is easy to become trapped. As if to accentuate this warning an adder suddenly slid across our path and we made haste to climb the little bank that separated us from the beach. Here we sat for a while in the sun listening to the innocent little waves gently lapping on the shingle and watching the yachts passing up and down the Solent in the deeper water. A very peaceful but thoughtful interlude.

Continuing our walk we climbed some steps cut in the bank at the back of the beach up through a fringe of trees and over a stile into the field beyond. The path took us alongside a wood on our left to another stile and we were then at the beginning of the saltings of the Newtown estuary. The foot-path across these marshes is very well marked and well constructed, and there are several wooden bridges and walkways to get you across dryshod. The path twists and turns, and obviously does not carry a lot of traffic for in the last field it crosses there were many patches of thistles and ragwort to be avoided along its route. The final stile brought us to Lower Hamstead, to an open beach with the old salterns to our left and ahead of us a rather rickety jetty built for the convenience of yachtsmen who land here to fetch water from Lower Hamstead Farm. At one time there used to be a small shop here selling groceries and other necessities, but this is now closed, and instead provides showers for campers.

To anyone interested in small boats this is a fascinating area for this is the Newtown River, the most beautiful and least spoilt harbour in the whole of the South Coast. It gets pretty busy nowadays at holiday times, for yachtsmen come a long way to savour its legendary peace and tranquillity, which nothing, not even a few dozen moored yachts can completely destroy. The very thought of a nuclear power station in this idyllic spot makes one shudder.

The entrance to the Newtown River from the sea is quite narrow, but once inside it spreads out into five separate arms, rather like the fingers of a hand. Each

A long wooden catwalk across part of Lower Hamstead marsh.

From the beach where the jetty comes ashore a lane runs up to Lower Hamstead Farm past a diminutive car park and a wood which hides a small and secluded National Trust camping site. We have many happy memories of this site since when our grandchildren were small we regularly camped here, this being an ideal spot for children who love camping and "messing about in boats". Just up the lane is another farmhouse, Creek Farm, which used to belong to a friend of ours and where we spent several weeks one summer looking after our friend's three cats while she was away sailing.

We continued on up the lane and after another half mile or so passed through a plantation of pines and rejoined the rough road leading up to Hamstead Grange, the road we had previously walked along. From here it was no distance at all to Pigeon Coo Farm and then another quarter of a mile back to where we had left the car. Re-invigorated from our walk we repaired to the Horse and Groom, a typical Island Pub on the main Newport to Yarmouth road, and one that is as good a place to sit and rest one's tired feet as any we know.

one is different and has its own charm. Its history has not always been peaceful, and indeed in the 13th and 14th centuries it was extremely turbulent. The town of Newtown and the harbour were built and developed by the Bishops of Winchester who owned the land, but Edward 1 took it away from them in 1285 and into Royal custody, since he was worried about a possible French invasion. His fears were ultimately realised for in 1377 the French landed in force and burned Newtown to the ground, having already destroyed the town of Yarmouth. Newtown was never rebuilt and has developed over the years into the haven of peace we enjoy today. Its continuation as such is due in very great measure to the National Trust who now own most of the area and have established it as a nature reserve.

Total Distance Walked: 3.3/4 miles

Did you know ?

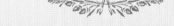

1   The saltings once supported a thriving industry in salt production, encouraged and developed by John Nash.

2   John Nash believed firmly in fostering local industries. He founded a brickworks at Hamstead and built a light railway to carry the clay from the pits near Lower Hamstead Farm.

3   His Shooting Box alas had to be demolished during the second world war as it became unsafe.

4   We saw more butterflies on this walk than on any other, particularly meadow browns, speckled woods, and hedge browns or gatekeepers. This was no doubt due to the profusion of ragwort, teasels, vetches, wild parsnip, and on the saltings great patches of sea lavender.

What to look out for

1   Pigeon Coo Farm, delightfully set among the trees.

2   Hamstead Grange stands in spacious grounds. A few metres before you reach the entrance gates there is a signpost. Stop here and look to the right, a vista over the Newtown estuary, once the proposed site for a Nuclear Power Station.

3   At the back of the Grange are some interesting old farm buildings, and a modern house on the site of John Nash's Shooting Box.

4   From the grove of pine trees you look down on the notorious Hamstead Ledge. Sometimes you can even see the water 'boiling' as it sweeps over the submerged shingle bank.

5   You can also see the remains of the war-time boom protecting the Solent and Spithead from enemy ships.

6   Note the Celtic Cross Memorial, almost on the beach, commemorating two separate tragedies by drowning.

7   Look out for one curious stile crossing the saltings, where the top beam has literally grown right inside the tree that supports it.

8   Note also the rather rickety jetty in the Newtown River used by yachtsmen who come ashore for water.

Walking Points

1   You may start this walk at the junction of Hamstead Road and the main Newport to Yarmouth Road, Map Reference 394894, or where we did, 1/2 mile further up Hamstead Road at 398901. There is a good bus service between Newport and Yarmouth.

2   The going is good all the way from the Yarmouth Road past Pigeon Coo Farm, Hamstead Grange, and down to the beach. The footpath across the saltings is well marked, but there can be muddy patches in bad weather.

3   The lane from the Lower Hamstead beach past the farm and Creek Farm can also be sticky at times.

4   Hamstead Estate roads are very rough, but robust wheel chairs could negotiate them with care and muscle, at least part of the way.

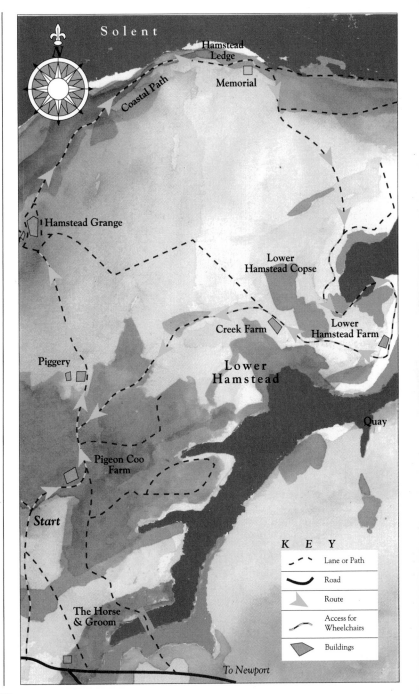

Amid the Alien Corn

There is an old saying that Life is full of surprises, and this applies to walks in unexplored country as well as to Life. One day, when we did not feel terribly energetic, and the weather did not seem able to make up its mind whether to rain or fine away, we decided on a short walk. A short walk, we said. A flat walk, we said. no toiling across rough ground or climbing steep hills, we said. A nice, gentle stroll in this glorious Isle of Wight countryside, so that we could return home pleasantly exercised and in no way exhausted. So we looked at the map.

Our choice seemed to fill all these requirements. We picked on a thinly populated part of the country bordering the valley of the River Medina where it flows through the Wilderness, just to the west of Godshill and the east of Chale Green. Half way along the road between the two villages is the start of a long straight, well defined bridleway to the north, its map reference being 502806.

We left the car at the beginning of this Bridleway No.11, which at this point is a good wide gravelled lane and is in fact a private road leading to North Appleford. The bridleway is well signposted, and there was plenty of room to tuck the car into the side out of everyone's way.

Our first surprise was a pleasant one, a very pleasant one indeed, for we found that the hedgerows on both sides of the track were full, and I do mean full, of wild flowers. The date was July 8th, and we had expected to find something of interest on our way, but were quite unprepared for the wealth of bloom bordering this modest little lane. Even as we got out of the car we

could see the brambles at this point covered in blackberry blossom, and we made a mental note to come back again later when the fruit would be ripe.

Now, wild flowers excite us. We cannot resist them nor pass them by without stopping to admire and possible identify them. Consequently our progress down this bridleway was very slow, and indeed it took over an hour to cover the first quarter of a mile. At the end of this time we were still in sight of the car, but had revelled in the many flowers we had seen, over 30 of which we had been able to identify.

One of the most outstanding was Mugwort, a tall plant with feathery leaves the undersides of which are silvery. Though the name is rather unromantic the plant itself is beautiful and the several clumps we saw were just about to burst into flower. Mugwort was the name given to it by the Saxons who regarded it as having magical and medicinal properties, and used it as a protection against lightning, the plague, carbuncles, and to repel midges. Quite a collection of useful qualities. The Latin name is artemisia vulgaris, Artemis being the ancient Greek goddess of the moon and a protectoress of women.

Another and even more versatile plant we came across was Burdock, a large branching thistle type plant with an almost incredible list of properties to its name, The juice was said to be a good antidote to the bite of snakes or rabid dogs, and to soothe burns and promote the flow of urine. The leaves were used on sores and ulcers, the seeds to combat sciatica, and the young stalks found their way into salads.

Apart from all these uses the seed heads when dry

Hedge Woundwort, Common Hemp Nettle and Betony

stick tenaciously to human clothing or animal skins, and this promotes distribution of the plant over a wide area. I can well remember as a boy having battles with my friends using these 'burrs' as missiles.

View across the cornfields towards Rookley.

The hedgerows contained many other plants we had often seen on other walks, agrimony, field scabious, campion, vetches, hedge woundwort, honeysuckle, field bindweed, willow herb, creeping cinquefoil, mouse ear hawkweed, foxgloves, nipplewort, bedstraw, cats ear, herb robert, black medoc, etc, etc, the list is almost endless. There were many varieties of thistle, spear thistle, creeping thistle, and black knapweed, and equally as many examples of the parsley family.

Non-botanists such as ourselves have difficulty in identifying all the various umbellifers, and even distinguishing between the harmless and the poisonous types. But there was much old and dead cow parsley about, and we thought we spotted hogweed, hedge parsley, hemlock, and a new one to us which we took to be angelica. This was a particularly beautiful young plant with delightful lilac coloured flowers. Along this stretch of the track also were many butterflies, tortoiseshells, red admirals, large and small whites etc. The tortoiseshells particularly settled on the ground in front of us, but before we could get close enough for a photograph they were off.

After a quarter of a mile we began to realise that if we were to complete the circuit in reasonable time we would have to get a move on. Fortunately the road

forked and changed character, the gravelled track shooting off to the left to North Appleford, and the bridleway continuing on to the right. From here there was less of hedge on our right hand side, only large fields, mainly of wheat, and the far side of these fields sloped up to Bleak Down. We sat down on the grass to drink our coffee, and ate a small snack for which we were to be very thankful later on. As we sat there an enormous hare came lolloping along the bridleway towards us. We sat very still, hoping he would come right past us, but inevitably I suppose he saw us, stood up for a moment to have a look, and then disappeared into the corn.

We discussed the many gorgeous flowers we had seen, made a few notes, and were agreed that so far we could confidently recommend this lane to anyone in a wheelchair who could be brought out here by car, or

Long headed Poppies amongst wheat, photographed near North Appleford Farm.

even by bus, for the going was good and smooth and flat, and there was much to see.

We set off again and continued along the bridleway, and soon we had our next surprise, but this was by no means a pleasant one, for the bridleway we were on suddenly came to an end. It looked almost as if it were turning to the right, which was not according to the map, but there was no sign of a way in that direction either, and ahead of us was a field of flax. The map told us that we had to continue across this field and that half way across the next field we should come to the footpath running from North Appleford on our left and taking us right across the field to Bleak Down. A tractor had already been through the flax in the direction we knew we had to go so we decided to press on through the unofficial path the tractor had made.

With hindsight we should have turned round at this point and gone back, but we had only walked about three quarters of a mile and were baffled by the fact that such a clearly defined bridleway should so suddenly and completely disappear. So we crossed the field of flax. The flowers were just going over but were still beautiful, and underfoot the tractor had left ridges on the ground and these did not make for pleasant walking.

The next field was wheat, and a very thick and healthy crop it looked too, but there was no bridleway. But the tractor had been across this one too, still in the same direction, so we carried on. We could see North Appleford buildings quite close on our left, and after only another 200 metres or so we came to a gate which led to the track up to the farm. But on this side of the gate no track at all, just wheat, right up to the hedge. But there was a signpost, peeping up out of the wheat, a signpost that told us we were still on the bridleway and that in fact this stretch was part of the Worsley Trail, one of the several excellent County Council cross country walks. But apart from the tractor runs it was quite impossible to walk it.

Again we missed the opportunity of turning back, but decided on a compromise. Instead of continuing any further in this direction we decided to take one of the many tractor trails leading across the field to Bleak Down, and though underfoot the going was very knobbly and uncomfortable, and we had to walk in single file, we agreed that if we took it easy with frequent stops it would not be too bad.

The first part of the field was flat and we crossed this fairly easily, but then the ground began to rise and the going got tougher. So we stopped frequently to rest, and found that there was a bonus, in that as we climbed higher each time we stopped the view behind was getting better and better. At the top was a hedge along which ran the vestige of a path, but this was one that had not been used for a long time. Behind the hedge was a narrow belt of scrub and we could hear the occasional traffic along the road beyond.

The Ordnance Survey shows this public footpath and so we followed it along the hedge, and after little more than a hundred metres came to a gate leading out through the scrub to the road. By this gate was a signpost, but alas the direction board was no longer at the top of the pole but was lying on the ground beside it, pointing in the wrong direction, but confirming that this was a public footpath and that its number was GL10. Through the gate we went and out on to the road, deciding that if the rest of the walk was going to be through fields of wheat, which had been so uncomfortable to the feet, we would be better off sticking to the road even though this lengthened the route and contained traffic hazards.

So off we set, but after only a few metres saw a gap in the hedge by the roadside and through this a carved wooden signpost announcing a public bridleway and pointing in the direction we wanted. The map shows this one too. We could see that the fields ahead were grass and not wheat, and so once again we changed our minds, as walking downhill on grass was much to

Painted Lady on Great Willowherb and Bramble

be preferred to walking on a road along which cars and lorries were occasionally thundering.

Our troubles were not over however, nor were the surprises finished, for though the fields were grassed, and infinitely preferable to walking through wheat, yet it was rather bumpy old grass and there was no definite sign of a bridleway. However, we knew the direction we needed to go and this was roughly parallel with a hedge on the right hand side. Perhaps our feet were beginning to get a little tired, and we were certainly grateful for the fact that it was slightly down-

Overgrown style, Bleak Down.

hill all the way. There were many rabbits in the field, and these scuttled back into the hedge bottom as we approached. We could see numerous rabbit holes and at one point a much larger burrow with a great mound of earth outside it. Was this, we wondered, a badger's sett, or a fox's earth? There were rabbit droppings all around and also some larger droppings, and not for the first time we regretted our ignorance at not being able positively to identify this.

After three quarters of a mile we came to Leechmore Farm on our left, and a little further on was the pond which gave the farm its name - for it means ' the mere, or pond, in which leeches are found'. In bygone times leeches were very important medicinally, and this pond, which was much bigger at the time of the Domesday Survey in 1086, was the Island's principal source of supply.

Total Distance Walked: 2.25 miles

It was difficult to see the pond until we were very close to it for it was surrounded by undergrowth and nettles, nettles, nettles. The latter are usually a sign of previous human involvement in times past, and for a moment it looked as though we were not going to be able to get through. But there was a wicket gate, which meant that there must be a path, and after literally fighting our way through head-high nettles and past a bay tree we reached a stile which led us on to the road. Here we found another carved wooden sign pointing the way we had come and announcing that his was indeed a public bridleway, but we must have been the first walkers to use it for many a long day.

Another quarter of a mile or so and we were back at the car, rather hot and tired and having taken so long over this short walk that we had missed our lunch. however, this loss was remedied by going into Godshill where at Essex Cottage we had a delicious cream tea in their very pleasant garden under a cherry tree.

While we recovered we discussed the salient points of the walk, which had been full of surprises and not a bit what we had expected. The first half mile had been perfect, and we would like to think that handicapped people who cannot normally get out into the countryside and enjoy the wild flowers would find it suitable and interesting. But for the rest of it we cannot really recommend it to anyone who is less than 100% fit. Farmers who plough up public rights of way possibly do not appreciate the effect this has on the rest of us.

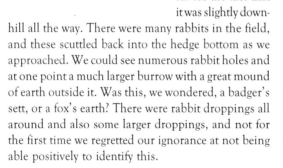

Did you know ?

The pond at Leechmore Farm is not very large, but it did give the farm its name and is hence worthy of note. Leeches were bred in this pond from time immemorial, and at one time were used extensively in medicine.

118

What to look out for

1   *Bridleway No. 11, Map Reference 502806, is full of wild flowers in summer, and to anyone interested in flora it is a happy hunting ground.*

2   *As well as so many flower species look out for the butterflies, we saw many red admirals, tortoiseshells, and large and small whites.*

3   *Look out also for hares in the wheatfields. We met one coming straight towards us.*

4   *Though not as spectacular as some, the views westwards across the Wilderness and the Medina Valley towards Kingston and Billingham are extremely pleasing.*

5   *Bleak Down is interesting for the views it affords, and also for the opportunity to get your breath back.*

Walking Points

1   *Easy to park a car at the beginning of the bridleway.*

2   *The first half mile is good walking and full of interest. In our opinion eminently suitable for wheel chairs.*

3   *When the track forks take the one to the right, for this is the public bridleway.*

4   *When the bridleway disappears you can still get through near the hedge on the left, but it may mean walking along tractor tracks. This is rougher going and you need to be fit.*

5   *A public footpath goes off to the left to North Appleford Farm and a signpost confirms this. One field later this footpath swings sharp right and crosses to the high ground at Bleak Down, this being part of the Worsley Trail. We found the corn distinctly alien. There was a signpost on Bleak Down, but this was on the ground in pieces.*

6   *Go out into the road at Bleak Down, turn right, and a few metres further on there is a gap in the hedge and another signpost pointing over a stile towards Leechmore Farm.*

7   *Leave the farm and the pond on your left and go through a gate into a thicket of head high nettles. On the other side of this a gate will let you out on to the road. Turn right, and a quarter of a mile later you will be back at the start.*

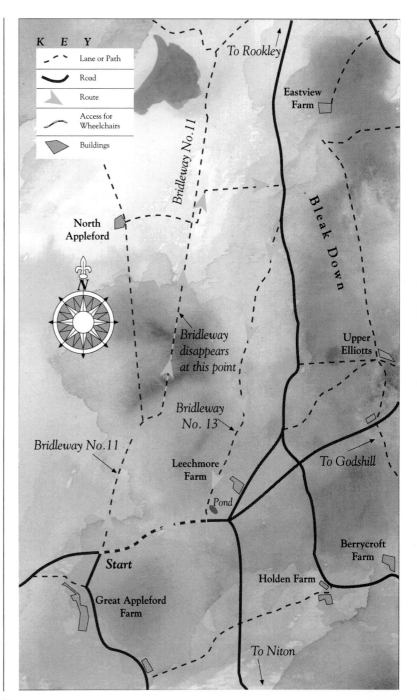

H and C

ot days are not really for walking, and when we suddenly decided, one blissful summer morning which promised a hot day ahead, to drop everything and go up on the downs, we wondered if we were being wise. Normally we like to plan our walks in advance, poring over the maps and working it all out in as much detail as possible, but there are occasions when the urge takes us to get away from it all and we just grab the maps and a flask of coffee, and go. And it has to be said that these occasional snap decisions seldom disappoint. This of course is one of the great advantages of being retired, and after years of leading a disciplined nine-to-five existence the ability to break out on the spur of the moment and throw one's bonnet over the windmill is nothing less than glorious.

On this particular day the sun rose about 5.30, appearing over the high ground to the east and flooding our bedroom with golden light, and though we did not get up immediately it was much too good to stay in doors for long. Out in the garden the stillness and peace was magical. There was a heavy dew on the lawn and as the sun climbed higher and the blue of the sky intensified, so the colours of the flowers strengthened and deepened and clamoured silently for attention. In our garden at this time of the year we have several clumps of yellow loose-strife in full flower, and these are great favourites of ours, particularly as next to them are purple and pink geraniums, the colour contrast being most satisfying.

It was obviously going to be a hot day, just the sort of day for pottering about in the garden and occasionally sitting in the shade. So I got out the garden furniture and put up the table with its umbrella, and went back into the house for breakfast. Which one of us actually suggested we should go for a walk I don't really know, and it doesn't matter, but when my wife said "There will be a nice breeze up on the Down" the adrenalin started to pump and that was it. She knows that the high Downs around Brighstone Forest and Gallibury Fields have a fatal fascination for me, so there was no more to be said.

We made for Rowridge. Along the Middle Road from Newport towards Freshwater until we reached Apesdown where we turned sharp left into Rowridge Lane. Had we been younger and fitter, or had it been cooler, we might have left the car here, for this little road is delightful to walk along and you really feel you are leaving the troubled world behind the further you go. It climbs steadily though not sharply for a little over a mile until near its end it swerves to the right and leads to a couple of houses and the T.V. Station with its huge mast that supplies the Island with its television programmes. We kept straight on however and into the farmyard of Rowridge Farm (Map Ref. 449862).

The farmhouse is a simple white painted building and its situation, to anyone who values peace and quiet, cannot be bettered. Set in a bowl of the Downs and sheltered on all sides, it is surrounded by woods and hilly fields and mile after mile of beautiful countryside, its only neighbours being the cluster of buildings round the T.V.Mast, which however are out of sight behind a wood. The young farmer and his wife readily and kindly gave us permission to leave our car in the yard and we tucked it away where it was out of sight and not likely to be a nuisance to anyone. The farm covers 420 acres and must be very difficult to work for

Cowslip

this is hilly country, and it was not surprising to learn that sheep, of which he has 1300, were his principal care.

There has been much controversy about the T.V. mast, and many letters written to the local papers, for the authorities have changed the lighting on it. Originally it carried a row of stationary red lights as a warning to aircraft, but these have been replaced by brilliant white flashing lights which can literally be seen for miles. This is indeed the age of flashing lights, they obtrude everywhere, and on the roads about one vehicle in every three now seems to carry one. At one time only the police had them, but now even the dust cart has to be thus equipped. No doubt this is merely a temporary fashion, a fad that will hopefully die out in due course along with other reprehensible customs such as drinking out of tins and bottles.

Pink campion on Swainston Down.

The first half mile was uphill, not a very serious climb but one that we took slowly, to begin with along the edge of a wood and then straight across a field containing many sheep. As we climbed higher the view behind us afforded a good excuse for frequent stops. Ahead of us on the skyline we could see a signpost and when we reached it we found that it was on a wide chalk track crossing the downs from south east to north west. Only a hundred yards or so along here we came to a cross roads by a large disused chalk pit and here we had to turn left.

This cross roads is clearly marked on the map and is named Swainstondown Gate, and this immediately excited our curiosity. Swainston is of course one of the most historic places in the whole of the Isle of Wight, dating back to Saxon times. At the time of the Domesday Survey in 1086 the manor of Swainston belonged to the Bishops of Winchester and was by far the largest and most valuable in the Island. One arm of the track from the cross roads we were at went directly to the manor house just over a mile away, and then on to Clamerkin Lake in Newtown Harbour. In the opposite direction, and this was the route we were now about to take, it ran for nearly three quarters of a mile before merging with the ancient Downs highway that crosses the Island from the Needles to Carisbrooke and beyond.

We were right about the breeze. Up here, on top of the world, there was unlimited sunshine, a clear blue sky, and the breeze, a steady Force 2, was cool and refreshing. We looked round us; to the north we could see the Solent, to the west the dark mass of Brighstone Forest, and to the south, the way we had come, the land was shimmering in the sun. To the east was a typical Isle of Wight landscape of undulating Downs,

Part of the fantastic view from the top of the world, looking north to the Solent.

fields and woods, that even the dominating presence of the immensely high T.V.mast did not spoil. We paused for a while to savour the scene, thinking how lucky we were to have all this beauty given to us, and to have the ability to walk the short distance necessary to reach such a heavenly spot.

On a more practical note we began to think of our flask of coffee, but decided to walk a little further and to reach at least half way before we sat down to rest. The next half mile or so brought fresh delights. The track was fairly level, running alongside the hillside towards Brighstone Forest, with stupendous views to our right. On the left the ground rose and alongside the track was a bank covered in brambles, wild rose, nettles, elder, and other hedge plants, and a wealth of wild flowers. Immediately we slowed down, for we find it quite impossible to pass flowers without stopping to admire them and trying to identify them.

On this bank were many clumps of Campion, both red and white, and also the equally beautiful but not so prettily named Bladder Campion. The scientific name for Campion is 'silene' from Silenus the ancient merry god of the woodlands, who with his happy and carefree, and sometimes drunken, behaviour enlivened the woods and hedgerows, and there is no doubt that the Campions do indeed brighten up their surroundings with their gay and carefree flowers. Also on the bank were patches of the yellow meadow vetchling and blue speedwell, the latter having long had a medical reputation for treating wounds and curing respiratory diseases, hence its name.

Other plants we saw and recognised were cow parsley, self heal, cowslips, hedge woundwort, greater stitchwort, and foxgloves. Stitchwort, incidentally, was so named for it was believed to be capable of curing a 'stitch' in the side and similar pains. The various woundworts too were highly regarded medically, particularly, as their name implies, for treating wounds and stemming bleeding. Underneath our feet in the grass verges of the track were many miniature plants including a tiny chickweed type flower and the brilliant miniature golden ball shaped flowers of the Black Medic, a plant with shamrock type leaves whose name has in fact nothing to do with medicine, but merely refers to its origin in the land of the ancient Medes. Towards the end of this stretch of the track, just before we reached the wood, we found on our right a large patch, several acres of it, covered in red and white campions and yellow buttercups, an unforgettable sight. In all it took us the best part of an hour to reach the edge of the wood, where we sank down gratefully on the turf to drink our coffee and take a last look at the fantastic view. The only discordant note at this point was the droning of several light aircraft high overhead, diving and climbing and disturbing the peace of the countryside for miles round. Why, oh why do they have to practice over the Isle of Wight when there is so much open sea available in the neighbourhood? We know we are not alone in this complaint for many other people have mentioned it to us and have found it very trying. Perhaps the airmen just do not realise that their noise can be heard over a wide area by hundreds, if not thousands, of people.

Before we got into the wood itself there was a band of scrub through which the track twisted and turned and in places dwindled to a footpath, and here the map ceased to be an accurate guide for it shows none of the various bends and off-shoots which we found slightly confusing. But the map did show a large tumulus that we passed, and an enclosure that had been, and apparently still was, under cultivation. Ultimately we entered the wood itself and found the junction with the ancient high way and a signpost showing the three directions - to Brighstone, to Ashengrove (near Swainston) and to Carisbrooke.

This was really the climax of our little expedition for we had walked this old road along much of its length between Carisbrooke and the Needles, but had never before trodden this particular stretch. This was also

Sweet Briar and Rosehip

the point at which we had intended to go no further west but to turn to the east and follow the highway back towards Carisbrooke for about a mile along the part we did not know. But we knew that we were only half a mile or so from the triangulation point high on Brighstone Down to the west, a point we knew well, so we decided to push on just that little bit further and see if we could reach it. The walk through the woods was delightful, there was plenty of shade and the going was level, though slightly muddy in places.

Tumulus at Map Reference 442854. Whoever is buried up here lies very close to Heaven.

However, we were still fresh enough to enjoy the walk of about a mile and a half back to Rowridge. At first this went back through the wood and then along its edge, and was in the form of a quite narrow footpath, which surprised us for we had been expecting a broad bridleway over its entire length. On the right of this path though was the remains of an exceedingly old hawthorn hedge, and it looked almost as if the original highway had been on the other side of the hedge. Soon we came out into the open and the old chalk highway was plain to see in front of us across the Down.

We continued along the highway in the direction of Carisbrooke for just over a quarter of a mile and reached another footpath to the left that would take us back to Rowridge Farm. Down this path we walked, dropping rapidly downhill and along the edge of Monkham's Copse, a wood we knew from previous walks. At the bottom of the hill the wood extends to the west and ends in a large and very old chalk pit

Total Distance Walked : 3.5 miles

which is now completely filled with trees. Back at the farm we received a boisterous greeting from the farmer's three Collie dogs, a father, mother, and son, all of whom are trained to work with the sheep. The dogs were friendly enough but I think an intruder up to no good in the dark would certainly have something to think about.

We had a friendly chat with the farmer and his wife who together with their two small children live in this idyllic spot, and must work very hard on such a hilly farm of this size. We were able to compliment him on one aspect of his husbandry, in that all his gates were well hung and readily opened and closed, thus making it easy for strangers to do the right thing We queried their use of what little leisure time they had, and were interested to hear that they seldom watched television, and that the children were not interested in it, simply because they had never been allowed just to sit in front of it and gawp at whatever happened to be on. What a refreshing attitude to find in young parents, and how much better we should all be by adopting a similar policy.

Thus ended a walk we shall long remember, partly because of the glorious weather, partly because of the incredibly beautiful landscapes and flowers we had seen, and partly because of the friendly people we had met. But mainly, I think, because all these individual factors when mixed together add up to what we call Happiness and Contentment.

Did you know ?

1 These old highways across the Downs were ancient when the Romans first came to the Island

2 Their P and Q (Peace and Quiet) have much to do with our H and C (Happiness and Contentment)

What to look out for

1 Rowridge Farm in its idyllic setting at the top of Rowridge Lane. The T.V. mast is impressive too.

2 Swainstondown Gate. On top of the world. Remote, Unbelievable. You might meet a medieval bishop, a nobleman, or a pedlar up here, and it would not be in the least surprising.

3 Between Swainstondown Gate and Brightstone Forest the views are magnificent.

4 What you will also see up here are wild roses, brambles, red and white campions, bladder campion, and many other wild flowers.

5 Note the large Tumulus at the point where Swainstondown meets the Tennyson Trail. What a splendid spot for a burial, and so close to Heaven.

6 If you like walking through woodland and downland these ancient highways are for you.

Walking Points

1 From Rowridge Farm set off up the hillside in a westerly direction.

2 At Swainstondown Gate crossroads turn left at the disused chalk pit on to a bridleway that runs for mile in a sou-westerly direction to Brighstone Forest, and joins the main ancient highway there.

3 Carry straight on through the wood for another mile or so to the Triangulation Point, or turn back along the highway towards Carisbrooke. This is the "Tennyson Trail".

4 1 mile along this trail to the east turn sharp left to get back to Rowridge Farm.

5 Throughout this walk the going is good, but hilly.

6 The surface of Rowridge Lane is smooth, and it is traffic free and delightful, but we hesitate to recommend it for wheel chairs on account of the gradient. You would need a very powerful "pusher".

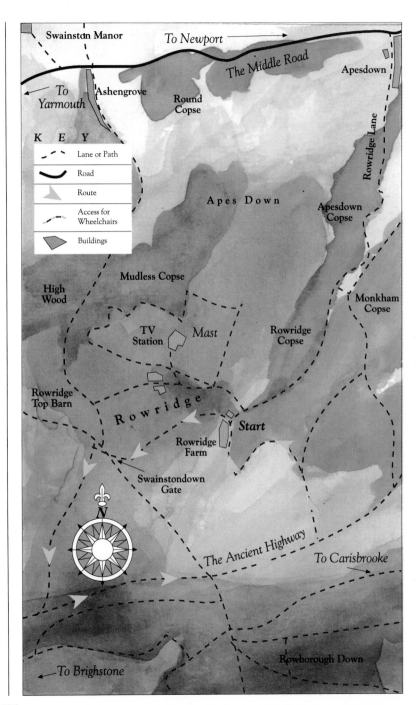

Swainston Manor
To Newport
The Middle Road
Apesdown
To Yarmouth
Ashengrove
Round Copse
Rowridge Lane
Apes Down
Apesdown Copse
Mudless Copse
High Wood
Monkham Copse
TV Station
Mast
Rowridge Copse
Rowridge Top Barn
Rowridge
Start
Rowridge Farm
Swainstondown Gate
The Ancient Highway
To Carisbrooke
N
To Brighstone
Rowborough Down

KEY

- - -	Lane or Path
⌒	Road
▷	Route
⌒	Access for Wheelchairs
◆	Buildings

Maps and Equipment

We do not claim to be Intrepid Travellers or Rugged Ramblers, but it is important to wear practical clothing when walking, and "sensible" shoes. Actually, we equipped ourselves with an Italian make of walking boots which are extremely comfortable and give good support, but which Pat found rather heavy. There are lighter makes available.

We used two types of map, both $2^1/_2$" to the mile. One was the Ordnance Survey Pathfinder Series and the other a pocket ramblers map published by the Isle of Wight County Council. Unfortunately, neither of these very convenient forms is now available, but the Pathfinder Series has been replaced by the Ordnance Survey Leisure Map No. 29, which covers the whole Island on one double sided sheet. This is a bit bulky, but is an excellent map. I doubt whether any other equipment can be regarded as vital, though a compass is advisable, just in case you lose your bearings. We also carried a Collins "Little Gem" book on wild flowers, a flask of coffee, and cameras, cameras, cameras. There is no prize for guessing who carried all this gear.

The Country Code

Keep your dogs under close control.
Keep to the public paths across farmland.
Use gates and stiles to cross fences, hedges and walls.
Leave livestock, crops and machinery alone.
Take your litter home.
Help keep water clean.
Enjoy the countryside and respect its life and work.
Guard against all risk of fire.
Fasten all gates.
Protect wildlife, plants and trees.
Take special care on roads.
Make no unnecessary noise.